MW00479611

JUST A LITTLE BIT MORE
THE HEART OF A MENTOR

Accounts of Cross-cultural Mentoring
and the Lessons they Hold

DR. BOB ABRAMSON

Alphabet Resources

Just a Little Bit More
Published by Alphabet Resources, Inc.
365 Stonehenge Drive
Phillipsburg, NJ 08865
1-908-213-2997
info@mentoringministry.com

Cover design by Ryan Stacey

10 digit ISBN 0-9843443-0-6
13 digit ISBN 978-0-9843443-0-7

Library of Congress Control Number: 2009944049

Contact Dr. Abramson by visiting
www.mentoringministry.com

"For this reason we also, since the day we heard it, do not cease to pray for you, and to ask that you may be filled with the knowledge of His will in all wisdom and spiritual understanding; that you may walk worthy of the Lord, fully pleasing Him, being fruitful in every good work and increasing in the knowledge of God;"

Colossians 1:9-10 NKJV

Corresponding Workbook Available

(Suitable for individual study or group training)

www.mentoringministry.com

info@mentoringministry.com

Alphabet Resources, Inc. 1-908-213-2997

CONTENTS

Preface ix

Introduction 1

1. An Unlikely Disciple 7
2. Expect the Unexpected! 25
3. They will Catch your Heart! 47
4. It takes a Father to Make a Son. 71
5. Landmarks in their Lives 95
6. How will you Answer the Rain? 117
7. Inconvenient Love 141
8. A Mentor's Guide to Survival 163
9. Transitions 189
10. Just a Little Bit More 209

Scripture Index 220

Preface

Just a Little Bit More

It was 1996. We had just arrived in the Fiji Islands[1] and were committed to be there for the next three years. My wife Nancy and I had visited twice before, but now we were to be embedded full time into a culture that was very different from what we were used to. We would pastor a church and establish a training school for ministry. We had great anticipation, but little understanding of this very special place with a very different way of living.

Our first Sunday, we were in services with the Christian Mission Fellowship church. It met in an old movie theater, which was in quite a state of disrepair. Long ago, it had been painted completely black on the inside. It looked like years had passed since any serious maintenance had been done. It was quite dirty. The day was typically hot and unbearably humid. The theater had no air conditioning and the air was absolutely still. It did not take long for all of us in the crowd to generate a less than pleasing odor.

Nancy and I were seated on the front row. We knew the whole service would be in the native Fijian language and we would not have a clue of what was going on. As the worship team began to sing, a very large speaker just in front of us was sending forth a blast of sound that was

[1] The Fiji Islands are an island nation in the South Pacific.

far beyond my comfort zone. In spite of the sound nearly blasting us out of our seats, and even though we could not understand a single word, it became apparent there was a strong presence of God. The heartfelt worship of the congregation made a powerful impression on me. Nevertheless, I was getting physically more uncomfortable by the minute, and began to wish I were anywhere else but there!

After about an hour of praise and worship, the time came for the sermon. The church had invited a guest speaker that day. He was an imposing-looking man who preached with great passion, but again, it was in Fijian. I had no idea what he was saying. I sat there sweating, wondering how long it would be until I could get out and go somewhere cooler. I thought to myself, "Lord, what am I doing here?" Quite unexpectedly, God answered me. As I sat there, resigned to the fact that I would simply have to endure the sermon without a clue about what he was saying, it happened. In the midst of a sentence, the preacher switched to English and said five words that struck me like a hammer. He said, "Just a little bit more." Then he went back to speaking Fijian. About three or four minutes later, he again switched to English, "Just a little bit more." He did this about a half dozen times during his sermon. They were the only words he spoke in English. To this day, I have no idea why, except that God had a life-changing message for me – "Just a little bit more."

These five words became part of me. They began to define my relationship with God, and they became the guiding principle for my strategies as a mentor and pastor. As you read the pages that follow, I trust you will gain a sense of what they mean to me and what they can mean to you. My prayer is that what I share with you will help you become "just a little bit more" like Jesus every day and in every way!

Introduction

"A great leader is not a man who does great things, but
a man who gets others to do great things."
(President Ronald Reagan)

(Matthew 28:18-19 NKJV) "And Jesus came and spoke to them, saying, "All authority has been given to Me in heaven and on earth. {19} "Go therefore and make disciples of all the nations, baptizing them in the name of the Father and of the Son and of the Holy Spirit,"

This is a book about the principles and dynamics of disciple making, or Biblical mentoring.[2] The process of mentoring is many things. On a practical level, it equips others to come away with greater competence, skill and motivation to do what they are destined to do. In its essence however, it is a process of loving and nurturing the people God assigns to us along the way to our destinies, and theirs. It is about our lives unfolding in ways that, by God's design, take us across the paths of others. These are not chance meetings. They are divine appointments and purposeful connections. When these occur, they become meetings marked with divinely intended consequences. They are often not encounters of our choosing, but they ultimately require that we make a choice - a choice to engage or not. If we choose to engage, the

[2] All references to "mentoring" will refer to Biblically directed Christian mentoring, which is engaged in to achieve the destiny and purposes of God for those involved.

encounters grow into relationships. And so, the mentoring process is birthed out of our recognition and acceptance that we have come upon somebody God asks us to connect with for a season, so He can change and equip them for an eternity. If we understand and execute this process correctly, those we engage will engage us. It becomes a two-way street. As we teach and train them, the experience becomes our teacher as well as theirs.

Mentoring: The intentional process of loving and nurturing people God assigns us along the way to our destinies

The pages that follow will introduce you to many of the people God has given me and my wife Nancy to mentor.[3] Out of the stories of their lives (and ours), I will present you with the mentoring dynamics and principles I have gleaned through my experiences. But this book is intended to be more than a "how to" manual on mentoring. It is a collection of brief narratives, illustrating the incredible grace of God at work through His loving, purposeful intervention in the lives of His people. Their stories will reaffirm the truth that with God all things are possible. Even in the most impossible situations, He will use our mentoring relationships to turn the blank canvasses of many lives into colorful, significant portraits of fully functioning people who find their strength and purpose in Him. There is much to be learned from the people you will meet on the pages that follow. Keep your heart open. God will speak through them, not just about mentoring, but about His graceful intervention and favor in the lives of those who dedicate themselves to following Him. You will read about the victories of people who found His strength in their weakness, His purpose in their willingness, and His love in the lives of those they touched.

---

[3] All reference to sons will include by default an assumed, unwritten and implicit reference to daughters. No prejudice or disrespect is intended. God gives mentors and disciples of both genders. The principles in the book remain the same for either.

I have no doubt that the people you will meet in this book will speak to you in ways that I never intended or expected as I wrote about them. Each is an inspiration and testimony to the goodness of God. Any one of them can become a source of revelation to you, as God speaks through their stories. I encourage you to look beyond what I have found and reported. Taste and see the goodness of the Lord. Enter into the vast reservoir of that goodness awaiting you. Then trust the Lord to use what you have discovered for His glory, as you mentor those He gives to you.

> *(Psalms 34:8 NKJV) "Oh, taste and see that the LORD is good; Blessed is the man who trusts in Him!"*

The book is a product of more than 20 years of ministry. It recounts experiences from Asia, the South Pacific and across America. Some of the identities of the people, details and places have been changed to protect their privacy and personal information. Some of what you read will take place in Suva, the capitol city of the island nation of Fiji, in the South Pacific. We found ourselves invited to come and serve on this particular mission field because there was a need for a ministry training school and an international church. Our time there was as meaningful as any we have ever experienced. The people of Fiji are very special and wonderful. The dedication of our Bible school students and our church congregation there was complete, and in many cases, completely sacrificial. It was a time when all our lives were forever changed. We came to mentor and Fiji ultimately mentored us. Our other significant places of ministry were in Asia and America. We have pastored in Florida and planted two international churches in New York City. The first was on Roosevelt Island, the second, several years later, in Manhattan and Queens. Though there were many nations and cultures represented in both church plants, the second church plant evolved into an overwhelmingly Chinese congregation. For Nancy and me, the City presented some completely new challenges to our missionary hearts and understanding. It was a unique place and perhaps an even more challenging and difficult mission field than our experience in Asia and the South Pacific. It was so different, yet the experiences of mentoring were much the same. From what I have seen in the places we have labored in, mentoring principles are largely universal, though the ways we practice them will be very much tuned to the local situation.

As you read through the pages that follow, I hope to show you how I discovered the ways God was working out His grace in my life. He enabled me to help some very special people grow in Christ and become all He designed them to be. I will try to convey what it means to have the heart of a mentor, and to walk in ways that become models for others - ways that open doors to divinely inspired relationships with those He gives us as students, disciples, and sons and daughters in the Lord.

Mentoring is a costly exercise. It is an exercise in profoundly personal sacrifice. In the process everyone changes. I have come to believe that in all the mentoring I have done, God was interested as much in the growth and change I would go through as He was for those I mentored. I have also come to learn to embrace change in myself, even as I demanded it in others. Change will demand determined personal effort and a willingness to go the extra mile - often requiring us to forsake comfort and security. Change is a beautiful thing. It is the perfect will of God.

Mentoring: A costly exercise in profound personal sacrifice, leading to growth and change - It is an open door to divinely inspired relationships.

(Romans 12:1-2 NKJV) "I beseech you therefore, brethren, by the mercies of God, that you present your bodies a living sacrifice, holy, acceptable to God, which is your reasonable service. {2} And do not be conformed to this world, but be transformed by the renewing of your mind, that you may prove what is that good and acceptable and perfect will of God."

A final thought before we move on to the first chapter - God will honor your willingness to mentor sacrificially, to give of yourself so that others may learn, grow, embrace and fulfill their destinies. In every mentoring journey, there will be surprises along the way. Some of your best surprises will be the unexpected rewards you will receive. There will be the rewards of seeing the true significance of your life, and of watching those you train discover the same for themselves. There will be rewards of warm fellowship as you grow to love those God gives you. There will be rewards of knowing how much you have changed in the process. There will be rewards of seeing the supernatural hand of God move into your life and make a way where there is no way. The greatest reward will be when you hear the words of our Lord, speaking with joy into your spirit,

"Well done good and faithful servant..."
(Matthew 25:23 NKJV)

I promise you, mentoring is well worth the price. Its rewards will bless you far beyond what it may have cost you.

What is Mentoring?

(From the thoughts and definitions given above)

Mentoring is the intentional process of loving and nurturing the people God assigns us along the way to our destinies. It is a costly exercise in profound personal sacrifice, leading to growth and change. It is an open door to divinely inspired relationships.

Chapter 1

An Unlikely Disciple

ꕥ Jeremiah ꕥ

It was a Sunday in New York City in the spring of 2003. We were pastoring a multicultural fellowship, meeting in a small hotel, close to Union Square in Manhattan. I had just finished preaching that day, and was beginning to pray for people, as I usually did at the end of the service. A woman in our church named Linda brought a Chinese couple forward for prayer. Jeremiah was a big, burly, gruff-looking guy, who was forty-seven years old. Sarah was a strikingly beautiful woman in her thirties. She spoke no English. I had never seen either of them before. As I stepped in front of them, and before anyone could say anything, I felt something deep on the inside. I simply spoke what I felt, saying, "God is going to heal your marriage." Jeremiah was shocked. A Mandarin speaking member of the congregation, who was interpreting for Sarah, told her what had been spoken. Sarah fell to the ground sobbing. I prayed for them and then the service was over.

After the service, I learned they had just signed divorce papers. Sarah was in a relationship with another man and Jeremiah had flown into New York to finalize the divorce. He was scheduled to fly back to Asia the next day. To this day, I have no idea how Linda convinced them to come to church together, but God had His plan and intervened in their lives as only He could. Jeremiah and Sarah had a divine appointment with Jesus. Their plans had been interrupted by God and the changes in their lives began to happen quickly. Despite threats on her life, Sarah cut all ties with the man she had been in relationship with. She and Jeremiah were drawn back together. They both started attending church services every time the doors were open. Their relationship began to heal. As individuals, and together they began to undergo incredible changes. Some months later I was delighted to perform a recommitment ceremony for their marriage.

When Jeremiah encountered God that first Sunday in our church, it was like lightning had struck. He was immediately infected with a zeal I have seldom seen. In fact, my initial impression was that his fervor was so great that it had to be phony - just a way to get his wife back. I kept looking at him with skepticism. I resisted him. I kept telling myself there was no way it could be real. However, as the weeks and months passed, I became fully convinced of the reality of his transformation. I could no longer resist him. Something in my heart kept urging me to take a risk and believe in him. This big, ungainly Chinese man, who had almost no knowledge of the Bible, began to serve in the church. He became a gentle, loving husband.

In the church, he would do whatever he could without being asked. He looked for ways to help and required nothing in return. He exhibited an unquenchable hunger for the Word and pressed me for answers to so many questions. I could hardly keep up with the sheer volume of questions he asked. I began to realize there was something extraordinary happening that only God could have initiated, but only Jeremiah could pursue. It was totally unexpected on my part. I am sure it was the same for him.

Jeremiah was, and still is full of the fire of God. He is completely given to his call to preach the Gospel. Perhaps I took the risk to embrace him as my disciple because he reminded me of where I was when I first met the Lord. I saw the same fire for Jesus burning in him that compelled me to take the road I have traveled. I saw him following his heart and I had no choice but to follow mine. It was once said to me that we should be careful who we give our hearts to, but we ought to give our hearts to someone. I took the risk. He became my disciple.

Take a risk. Open your heart!

We began to meet together weekly at a diner in Queens for one-on-one mentoring. I knew these were special times. I always came prepared to pour out my heart to him about my Christian worldview, and used the time to teach him the principles and practices of Christian ministry. He came each time with many questions. We discussed issues and topics of all kinds. It was productive and enjoyable for both of us. We used the time to cement our relationship. It became very solid. Jeremiah also enrolled in the evening Bible school I was running. There, he learned exegesis and hermeneutics. I was determined that he would establish a correct, balanced and efficient knowledge of Bible study methods. I asked him to write sermons and each week he would come to our house with them. Nancy and I would listen and critique him. He received this with great appreciation, and accepted the criticisms and corrections with humility. We discovered he had a strong and rather unique preaching gift. He was a natural storyteller and his one-liners were riveting. It gave me great joy when the time came for Jeremiah to step behind the pulpit for the first time to share the Word of God. God had given him a gift and he worked diligently to perfect it. He began to speak at cell group meetings. People would seek him out for counsel. He became my liaison and interpreter for those in our congregation who only spoke Chinese. God was giving him great exposure to ministry within the safety of our church and my supervision.

As time went on, I publicly acknowledged Jeremiah as a leader in the church to whom people could turn. This was more a recognition of what he was already doing than an attempt to get them to turn to him. And so, in these times of his early ministry, he was thrust into the lives of others. These encounters drew him closer to the cross. He was challenged by his opportunities, his relationships, and by me. Most of all, he was challenged by the Holy Spirit to discover the true impact and value of love, mercy and grace.

By that time, Sarah was being mentored by a godly Chinese woman in our church. She too was filled with zeal and fire. Her transformation was no less amazing than Jeremiah's. Even though we could only communicate with her through an interpreter, Nancy and I felt her love for us and our hearts were knitted together. She would often cook us wonderful Chinese dumplings and soup. We never saw her without receiving hugs and smiles. Nancy found one particular way to break through the language and cultural barrier. When she saw Sarah, she would teach her an English expression and Sarah would teach Nancy the same in Mandarin. They would laugh together as each struggled to pronounce words that did not seem to fit their mouths. God was at work.

It was not long before Jeremiah expressed to me his desire to go back to China and wherever else God would send him to preach the Gospel. When Jeremiah left for China, ours became a long-distance relationship that continues at the time of this writing and will probably last until one of us, one day, goes to meet Jesus!

The time and effort I invested in Jeremiah was not always convenient or easy. There were cultural gaps between us that only the Holy Spirit could bridge. Often I found myself relying on my love for him and his family to get our mentoring relationship through the rough spots. In this relationship I saw the manifestation of the truth in 1 Corinthians 13:8 that "love never fails." (The Chinese bible interprets this verse as "Love is eternal.") Love enabled me to do what I had to do to help Jeremiah begin the long climb toward competency in his Christian walk and ministry. Love gave me patience and helped me to see him as my brother, and even eventually as a son. (He was the most unlikely son I could ever imagine.) He would carefully consider what I was saying or teaching. At times, he struggled with what I said. In the end, he consistently came around. God was moving within him in a wonderful way. I am thankful that he learned to value my counsel. I believe it had more to do with his recognition of the reality of my care and concern for him and his family, than all the weight of my theological degrees and experience. Jeremiah was truly transformed through the process of mentoring. He understood the value of the Word and wisdom of God... and especially the love of God. He willingly received what I offered. He devoured it and became the classic learner under discipline. He became a disciple I will always be proud of. He became "just a little bit more like Jesus!"

In their second year with us, a son Daniel was born to Jeremiah and Sarah. They are some of the best parents I have ever observed. Even as an infant, Daniel loved to be in church. He was soon raising his hands and praising the Lord. When I would preach, he loved to wander up and stand, looking at the microphone, just wishing he could grab it and do the same. Daniel is a gift from God, not just to his parents, but to all of us who were in the church. He was birthed out of the grace that can only come from reconciliation in Christ.

Near the end of Jeremiah and Sarah's stay in New York I felt it was time for them to move on to China. Jeremiah continued to express how strongly he felt about doing so, but he said he was waiting for the right moment. I was sure that he and Sarah were ready and that it was time. We would discuss this frequently, but I had been careful not to try to influence him unduly, as to the timing of their departure. I wanted him to hear from God and leave with a firm conviction and strong anticipation that great things awaited him. Yet, he remained reluctant to go because he was looking for what he considered would be a sure, undeniable indication it was time to go. I was frustrated with his hesitation. He was entrenched in his need to receive an almost audible word. It was as if he was looking for the finger of God to write his ticket to China physically on the wall! Finally, at the close of one Sunday service, while praying for people, I could no longer contain myself. Looking back, I am certain it was the Holy Spirit compelling me to speak. I blurted out, *"Jeremiah, "Go to China!" It is time."* I had not intended or expected that to come out, but it did.

Jeremiah immediately went into denial. Even though he was perfectly aware of the call on his life, and had a fiery commitment to it, he found himself in a struggle. He knew it was time to leave, but found himself fighting a war in his flesh. Life in the church and in New York City was pleasant for him and a blessing for his family. Departing would mean great change and risk taking. He struggled with the words I had spoken to him. I watched as he fought to embrace the reality of the moment. A couple weeks went by during which he had no peace. Finally, he came to me. He apologized for not receiving and accepting what I had said at the close of that Sunday service. He said that he had meditated on it, wrestled with it, but no matter what he did, it would not leave him alone. Finally, he accepted it. It became the open door to his destiny. And so it was shortly thereafter we laid hands on him, ordained him, and sent him out to the will of God. He and his family flew to China.

At the time of this writing, Jeremiah, Sarah and Daniel have been living in China for over a year. I communicate with him regularly by email and occasionally by phone. What has happened in his life and ministry is nothing short of miraculous. God's hand is mightily upon him and his family, even as their mission in China has only just begun. Jeremiah sends me scores of accounts of miraculously changed lives in China. He recently sent a message, reporting that he had baptized his first thirty-five people. His great and simple faith in God is amazing. His life is a living epistle of what we all ought to strive for, to simply live a life of trusting God.

What is Mentoring?

Throughout this book, we will try to answer this question. To begin with, mentoring goes far beyond the act of teaching, though it must include teaching, along with great amounts of one-on-one dialogue. Mentoring is not a training regimen, though it requires a disciplined course of action, with enforced accountability. It is not a program, though it needs to have a structured design, which leads to a desired and highly focused end. Mentoring is not simply a skill, though, like a skill, it must be learned and practiced. I would categorize it as a craft, carefully learned, relearned and practiced.

Mentoring: A carefully learned, relearned and skillfully practiced craft

At its core, mentoring is a steadfast dedication to a heartfelt, committed, ever-growing one-on-one relationship. It is a season of walking together, teacher and pupil, father and son or mother and daughter. People who answer the call to mentor will only succeed if they can exemplify the ageless model of Christ with His disciples. Mentoring, for Jeremiah and me, was the acceptance of our mutual responsibility before the Lord to love and care for each other. Mentoring was my opportunity to plant seeds in the soil of a life very different than my own, knowing all along that it would not be my harvest to reap. Harvest is another season for another place. Harvest never belongs to the planter. It always belongs to the King.

I would have to release everything about Jeremiah's future service. It belonged to the Lord. I now have the satisfaction of knowing that the seeds of my mentoring are blossoming within a man who is finding his place in the Kingdom of God. He will do great things for God, most of which I will never know of this side of heaven. Jeremiah's life will glorify the Lord.

Mentoring: A season of planting in the good soil of lives that bud, blossom, bloom and grow

As I look back at my time with Jeremiah, I can easily see that the dominant factor in the mentoring process was our relationship. It had its challenging moments. Any time two people enter into the bond mentoring offers, they will find loads of opportunities for disagreement, discord and strife. Jeremiah and I were able to overcome these moments because we both recognized our commitment to each other and to what God was doing between us. Jeremiah knew that I was trying my best to go beyond teacher and become a father-like one to him. I knew he was doing his best to stretch himself. I knew he appreciated what was in my heart and wanted whatever it was he saw at work in me. In time, we became very close and cared a great deal for each other, not just as mentor and disciple, but as brothers in the Lord. We both learned the value of the people God gives us to walk together with. I am sure if you ask Jeremiah, he will tell you I was his gift from God. That is surely my confession about him.

I rejoice that the reports I receive from China indicate that others are now drawn to Jeremiah, much as he was drawn to me. Now it is his turn to make disciples. He is immersed in the will of God for his life. He has begun the mentoring process with these new people God has given him. I know in my heart that a little piece of me is forever in him, and in some small measure, I am there with Jeremiah, taking China for Jesus!

Mentoring: A steadfast dedication to a heartfelt, committed, ever-growing one-on-one relationship

> *(2 Timothy 2:1-2 NKJV) "You therefore, my son, be strong in the grace that is in Christ Jesus. {2} And the things that you have heard from me among many witnesses, commit these to faithful men who will be able to teach others also."*

I profited so much because of my time with Jeremiah. Most of it had to do with understanding the incredible worth of the people God gives us to love, train, encourage and care for. Such precious people become some of the greatest gifts God will ever give us. Jeremiah, Sarah and Daniel touched my heart in ways few others have.

I would like to share with you the three foundations of mentoring Jeremiah and others have taught me. These foundations are; (1) communication; (2) communion; and (3) participation and partnership (which together are really inseparable parts of one issue).

Communication

Mentoring is all about communication between mentor and disciple. Clear, concise communication is an acquired skill that none of us is born with. We acquire our communication patterns, habits and skills along the way. The need to communicate is paramount to the success of the mentoring process. Weak communication skills quickly render the mentoring process ineffective. They breed misunderstanding of purpose, intention and direction. Strong communication skills enable mentoring to work because they make for understanding. Understanding breeds change and change is what mentoring is all about. Our abilities to communicate with our disciples will depend on our prior training experiences, cultural awareness, skills with language and personal attitudes.

During the time I mentored Jeremiah, I often found understanding him required a great effort. It was not so much that his English was difficult for me to comprehend. He had good command of the language. However, I quickly learned that his thinking was flavored by his upbringing and life in Asia. It was my need to understand how he was thinking that could be so frustrating. His thought processes were very different from mine. I could not make assumptions about what he said out of my own experiences with life. I had to try to understand where he was coming from, so I could comprehend what he was communicating to me. I had to put myself in his shoes, as much as it was possible for someone so very different from him. This took the consistent exercise of patience. I realized early on, that I would have to zone in on him when he spoke to me and concentrate on hearing more than just his voice. I would need an open mind and a patient, humble heart. I would have to welcome and rely upon the guidance of the Holy Spirit. This usually required an attitude check on my part and often a serious adjustment. The moment would require that I escape my own a-priori assumptions about Jeremiah.

Like many of us, I am a better speaker than listener. I was constantly challenged as I struggled to accurately receive the thoughts and intents behind his words. When I remembered to assume very little, I found I would gain a great deal of understanding. Then, I was able to interact effectively with him. Jeremiah was faced with the same challenges and struggles. He handled them well. I would like to share with you four mentoring truths I learned from communicating with Jeremiah.

1. The need to <u>communicate clearly</u> is paramount to the mentoring process.

   Do not make quick and unmeasured assumptions about either your disciple, or the meaning behind the words he or she has spoken to you. When two people share their words, they must overcome two obvious blocking points to successful communication. The first point comes when a person chooses which words he will speak. As the speaker, he instinctively chooses and arranges his words in ways that are understandable to himself. His assumption (often a false one) is that the listener will correctly interpret the choice of words he has made. The task then, is to consider our choices of words and their construction into sentences with a concern that the person we are teaching will clearly comprehend them.

   The second obvious blocking point occurs when we are the hearer, not the speaker - when we receive what someone else is speaking. If we routinely accept their words to mean only what our own prior experiences and assumptions have established for us, we may not get through this blocking point. It is not natural for us to put ourselves in the minds and circumstances of the speaker while trying to understand what they are saying. The task therefore, is to approach our conversations with care, trying to hear more than just the words - in a sense, trying to read between the lines. This is an enormously useful mentoring skill. We are to try to hear the heart of the speaker. We must routinely give our own thinking room to adjust and expand. Assume little and you will learn much. Good communication occurs when both speaker and hearer exchange roles in their conversations with global, open and humble perspectives. In these contexts, mentoring has its chance to work.

Assume little and you will learn much!

---

2. The need to communicate will demand that we give priority to becoming better listeners.

   We touched on this in the paragraph above. The point to be made here is that we must have a primary awareness and desire to hear what is being said. We gain the power to do this from having a sense of compassion toward the other person. If we are to be good communicators, we must place a higher significance on listening to the other person's words and issues rather than on speaking what we feel is important at the moment. When we defer to the other person in this way, what we thought was right and important to say may change or even become irrelevant.

3. The need to communicate will test your patience and reveal your own heart to you.

   (Romans 15:5 NKJV) "Now may the God of patience and comfort grant you to be like-minded toward one another, according to Christ Jesus,"

A mature, effective mentor consistently strives to exercise control over his attitudes and emotions, and carefully measures his words. Control means patience, and patience is the protective umbrella over our frustrations and failures along the mentoring road. Patience prevents us from unmeasured, quick emotional responses. These invariably lead to disruptive, wrong or hurtfully negative words.

Patience also gives us the opportunity to look beyond the moment and into our own hearts. At these times, God gracefully allows us to find the hard spots. These become a mentor's teachable moments where we examine ourselves and allow the Holy Spirit to instruct us in God's righteous principles. These are times of victory and growth.

By injecting patience into our communications with our disciples, we become dispensers of forgiveness, mercy, understanding and compassion (components of God's grace). As a result, we form stronger, more successful connections. They become connections of greater intimacy and trust. As a result, both mentor and disciple grow in maturity.

4. The need to communicate is facilitated through applied grace.

It takes grace on our parts to communicate successfully with our disciples. For this to happen, we must seek and release God's grace in our hearts before we can project it onto theirs.

Grace is never to be taken for granted. I find myself constantly having to remind myself to soften my heart and give grace to others. My suspicion is that we are all in this category. Thank God

He never looked at us with judgment, but always was ready to shower us with grace. Thank God for the cross. Thank God for the grace Jesus had to endure it! We are saved by grace. We are given new beginnings by grace. We have God's favor by grace. How much more should we give what we have received to those incredibly valuable people God has given us?

Have you ever thought about what grace really is? In the mentoring process, we all face the opportunity to experience its flow between us and those we mentor. I am amazed at what mentoring continues to teach me about God's grace. It is not an easy thing to express, but let me give it a try.

Grace is all the goodness of God, the expression of His limitless, unbounding love, just waiting for you. God releases it in your time of need. It need not be earned, for it is His freely given gift. It is what you could never do for yourself and only He could do for you. It is sufficient for any circumstance. It is most often expressed through one person to another.

Grace is based on the quality of God's loving character. Grace draws you closer to Him, placing you under His protective, nurturing presence, under the shadow of His wing (Psalm 91). Grace gives you the limitless benefits of His presence and power. It is the perfect expression of the agape-love of God, which is fully validated and eternally insured by the blood of Jesus (its ultimate and eternal expression). And here is the most amazing thing about grace. It is almost always expressed through one person to another. It is seldom a sovereign act of the Lord without any connection to other people. This happens because grace is found in our God-given ability to do what we need to do, what we ought to do and what we get to do! It is the engine of divine empowerment that drives us to our destinies.

(Ephesians 2:8-9 NKJV) "For by grace you have been saved through faith, and that not of yourselves; it is the gift of God, {9} not of works, lest anyone should boast."

The mentoring process produced a lot of grace in both Jeremiah and me. It changed the way we communicated (not just with each other, but with others too). It made us more able, and willing to walk in each other's shoes. Our relationship grew progressively stronger because we got past many of our personal barriers to communicating with understanding. The graceful quality of our communications enabled the mentoring process to have a safe, secure and effective place in our lives. Communicating with grace was a key to our successful time together.

Communion

A biblically based mentoring relationship is always threefold - mentor, disciple and most importantly, the Lord. In the process of progressing in their relationship with each other, both mentor and disciple will experience countless opportunities to commune with each other on a high spiritual level. To commune implies an intimacy that goes beyond simple communication. It speaks of deeper levels of understanding and experience. This comes out of shallow beginnings, but if both submit to the leading of the Holy Spirit, it becomes the deeply enriching and edifying experience God intends it to be. Mentoring has the potential to go beyond communication and become communion when it touches both mentor and disciple with deeper things from the heart of God. This happens when they walk together in an ever-deepening communion with Christ. Jeremiah and I found that, though we are now thousands of miles from each other, we continue to walk together. Our communion with each other helps us to carry on our shared communion with Christ. It has taken us to places in Him we have never visited before.

Your disciples will take you to places in Christ that you have never visited before!

Participation and Partnership

The mentoring journey works best when the model the mentor creates for his disciple is not rigid, but has built into it a measure of flexibility. Mentoring is not like pouring wax into a fixed form, where each subsequent casting duplicates the previous ones. Flexibility and openness are qualities that every mentor and every disciple needs.

I have found in my mentoring experiences, that each season has been unique. For the most part, I have tried to go beyond the prideful error of thinking I might be the deciding factor - the instrument of change. It is God who brings the change, and the change occurs in both mentor and disciple, as they participate together as partners in the process. Success demands that both mentor and disciple consistently say, *Not my will but yours, Lord.*

God will be the deciding factor in the mentoring process.

An accurate picture of this process of participation and partnership is the image of two walking in agreement. There must be agreement about many things at many moments in the mentoring season. The overriding consideration is agreement that God will be the deciding factor in the process. This requires mutual respect and submission to the idea that we are part of a threefold cord, with the Holy Spirit as the dominant, binding One. Under His guidance, both mentor and disciple yield to Christ's command to love one another just as if we were loving ourselves. In all this, the hierarchy of spiritual authority is at work. The disciple becomes a follower of the mentor, and serves him appropriately.

> *(Ecclesiastes 4:9-12 NKJV) "Two are better than one, Because they have a good reward for their labor. {10} For if they fall, one will lift up his companion. But woe to him who is alone when he falls, For he has no one to help him up. {11} Again, if two lie down together, they will keep warm; But how can one be warm alone? {12} Though one may be overpowered by another, two can withstand him.* ***And a threefold cord is not quickly broken.****"*

The mentoring process is a walk that imitates the way Jesus walked with His disciples. It incorporates all the elements of participation and partnership that we glean from the four Gospels. Study the Gospels and you will see that the Lord formed His band of followers by building strong personal relationships with them. This is a picture of agreement and imitation. We imitate Christ and follow His mentoring example with our disciples. Each of us will have to define for ourselves what this will look like. Bear in mind that mentoring efforts will only be effective to the degree that we imitate the Biblical example of Christ. It is not so much about how we do it, but more so, about who we are when we do it!

Mentoring: Commitment to a special relationship in which communication, communion, participation and partnership all contribute to a process of imitation, which results in growth and maturity in Christ

Looking back, I have seen that each time I was given someone to travel the mentoring journey with, there was a uniquely graceful and divinely empowering experience awaiting us both. I always ask myself, *Where must this relationship take us?* I am conscious that there is a God-ordained destination for us. The mentoring journey may not be convenient or to our liking. Sometimes it can be a real pain in the neck! However, it invariably becomes a journey of light, illuminated with God's intention to lead us to a certain place and a moment in time, where it then ends with a fork, leading to two directions. From there, we continue apart from each other, assured that our paths will remain parts of a landscape far bigger than either of us.

What is Mentoring?

(From the definitions given in the pages of this chapter, above)

Mentoring is a carefully learned, relearned, and skillfully practiced craft. It begins with a season of planting into the good soil of lives that bud, blossom, bloom and grow. It is a steadfast dedication to a heartfelt, committed, ever-growing one-on-one relationship.

Mentoring is commitment to a special relationship of grace, in which communication, communion, participation and partnership all contribute to a process of imitation by those we mentor. This results in growth and maturity in Christ.

Chapter 2

Expect the Unexpected!

> *(1 Corinthians 4:15 NKJV) "For though you might have ten thousand instructors in Christ, yet you do not have many fathers; for in Christ Jesus I have begotten you through the gospel.'*

Suva is the capitol city of the Fiji Islands in the South Pacific. We were invited there to establish a ministry training center (which became known as The School of Urban Missions) and to pastor an international, English speaking church. We arrived there at the invitation of an indigenous denomination, the Christian Mission Fellowship (CMF).

We began the training center in a lean-to at the edge of what was at the time, the CMF headquarters. Our classroom was a primitive structure, with plywood walls and a corrugated metal roof. It was steaming hot and there was very little ventilation. When it rained, the noise on the tin roof was so loud I had to stop teaching until it subsided. It was a far cry from the typical American classroom I was used to. After about a month, I came to the sudden realization that my students had not understood most of what I had been teaching. In the typical American style, I had been speaking much too quickly and using words they were unfamiliar with. English was my students' second language and they had limits to their English vocabulary. Despite the fact that they couldn't understand, not one of the students had said a word to me about it. Why hadn't anyone spoken up? I was about to have the first of many cross-cultural learning experiences. I learned that the Fijian culture is very, very, gracious. Politeness is observed to a fault. There are unspoken cultural rules about what you can say, how you can say it, and who you can say it to. There is absolutely no place for correction of someone in a position of authority. They would never have said anything to me about their inability to understand my teaching. They just sat there and tried their best. When it finally dawned on me that they were not getting what I was trying to give them, I slowed my words down and tried to become sensitive to my use of vocabulary. As I taught, I watched, listened and did my best to read between the lines. I became a learner as much as a teacher. I began to study the Fijian language and did all I could to find out about their culture and its particulars. I had finally understood and embraced the most basic missionary requirement - I had to understand before I could be understood. I had to be a student of my pupils, before I could be their teacher. I had to observe, listen and learn, before I could understand how to communicate with them successfully. Communication would be the key. I might eventually do many things well, but they would all revolve around my ability to communicate.

Once the school was well underway, and I had been immersed in Fijian culture for about six months, it came time to assume the pastorate of the CMF's English speaking church service. The first Sunday that I was going to take the position as their new pastor, Nancy and I were given the address of the hotel where they met. We took a taxi to the hotel, not knowing what to expect. Where in the hotel would the meeting room be? What would it be like? I had certainly been in enough church services in hotels in America. So I thought I had a feeling for what we might encounter. When we got to the hotel, we found it was a multi-story building on a hill, looking over downtown Suva. We walked into the lobby and inquired as to whe. the church was meeting. They did not direct us to their meeting room. Instead, they told us to go next door to the bar that was attached to the hotel. When we walked in, it was quite an unexpected sight. The bar was painted black, including the ceiling and the floor. It reeked of the previous night's beer. I remember looking at the brightly polished mirrored ball hanging from the ceiling. A bar hardly seemed like a place where God might show up. Our small beginning of a congregation was anxiously awaiting our arrival and we were quickly ushered to the front row of chairs. My quick visual inspection revealed that there was a swimming pool just beyond where the worship team was set up. My first thought was that this would be great for baptisms. It didn't take long however to figure out that the children of the church had a different idea. After fishing a couple of them out of the pool one Sunday, a new ministry position of "pool guard" was quickly established. Expect the unexpected!

In due time, and with God's grace, our congregation began to grow. We began praying specifically for a facility in the heart of the city. One day as we were walking through downtown, we noticed an empty space in a building above some shops. This building was not only centrally located, but when we looked up on the face of the building we saw a sign. It was painted just above what would eventually be our windows on the second floor. The sign read, "In the Heart of the City." Nancy and I were amazed. We knew it was God. We knew it would be ours. The Lord can be very specific in response to our prayers. God intervened miraculously (a story for another time), and shortly thereafter we moved into the somewhat worn but large, brightly lit, inviting space. It took some work, but soon, both our young growing church and ministry training school were in full operation there. It was seldom empty or dark. The presence of God rested continually within.

People were constantly drawn to it. Often, when there was no scheduled activity for the facility, Nancy and I, walking by, would look up into the windows and see people gathered together. At times we would climb the stairs and open the doors to see handfuls of people, sitting in circles on the floor, just hanging out and fellowshipping or praying together. It was a place and a season ordained by God, in which He touched us all with His presence and His purpose.

Our church had a group of young men in their early twenties who were full-time church workers in training. They were fresh, young and excited. They were beginning to prepare for careers in ministry and the church was their training ground. They would live with and work under the guidance of my newly appointed associate pastor, whose name was Emitai. He was a seasoned Fijian missionary, and a student in the School of Urban Missions. We will learn more about him later.

I would be pastor, teacher, father, disciplinarian and mentor to Emitai and these young men for our season together in the South Pacific. It would be my responsibility to assure they were learning and growing in the right direction. Eventually, along with Emitai, they moved into a house loaned to our church for them to live in. It was right across the street from where Nancy and I lived. During those times when they were not in church or out and about the city performing their many and varied duties, they were just a shout away.

It did not take long to realize that these extraordinary young men were very special gifts to me. I quickly became their hero and they were a real challenge to my sense of humility. They thought I was Superman! They really never knew how much they were my heroes. They were always there for us. We could depend on them any time for anything.

It was beyond what we could have imagined. Their devotion to us and the church was immediate and uncompromising. They aimed to please! Their presence was an unusual exercise of the favor of God toward us. I could hardly believe our good fortune. We were surrounded by eager, untried young warriors, just waiting for the command to charge hell with nothing but their innocence and the untested strength of their faith. What an opportunity! What a responsibility! What a joy! When God challenges you with young warriors, do not neglect to make the commitment to love and care for them, to nurture and mentor them. They will bless you in so many ways it might just overwhelm you!

I struggled with how to approach my opportunity to shape these young warriors. I had definite ideas about discipleship, but to have interns as devoted, willing and gifted as these was new mentoring ground for me. They were captive subjects. Each was eager and willing. I would have to get it right. I needed to create a set of meaningful goals for them, from which I could design our mentoring journey together. I had to determine how to make these goals become reality. The significance of their lives was (at least for that season) in my hands. My thoughts went back to the Apostle Paul's prayer in Colossians 1:9-10. I recalled that his prayer was a foundational thread running through one of my most influential seminary courses. The course was all about individual, personal discovery of who we are in Christ, and its effect on how we mature in ministry. My thoughts and prayers, my goals and dreams for these young men would be no different than the Apostle's were for his Colossian friends.

> *(Colossians 1:9-10 NKJV) " For this reason we also, since the day we heard it, do not cease to pray for you, and to ask that you may be filled with the knowledge of His will in all wisdom*

and spiritual understanding; {10} that you may walk worthy of the Lord, fully pleasing Him, being fruitful in every good work and increasing in the knowledge of God;"

I took a fresh look at these two verses. From them I set four mentoring goals for my young disciples. I promise you, if you pray these four goals and do your part as God directs, you will significantly affect your disciples and their journeys toward the will of God. Here were my goals:

1. That they would walk worthy of the Lord
2. That their lives, their character and their hearts would be fully pleasing to Him
3. That their every good work would be fruitful - that their efforts would make a difference for the Kingdom of God
4. That each of them would progressively increase in the knowledge of God, causing them to be more like Christ in character, word and deed

These four goals could not be solely realized by what was taught. They had to be achieved by what was caught, and they had to catch it from me. My mentoring efforts would have to fulfill the Apostle Paul's words, that they (and in the process, me too) would *"be filled with the knowledge of His will in all wisdom and spiritual understanding."* Out of this prayer, I formed some boundaries for myself. If anything about my mentoring could not contribute to these four requirements, I would consider it invalid and would have to reject it. The challenge was clearly on my shoulders. What could I do? What should I do? What must I do? More importantly, what must I be, in this walk with my young men, for this season of our lives? I needed to discover the answers. They would dictate my methods and define my boundaries. Somehow, I would have to make an effort to become the closest thing to Jesus they had ever met. That was a scary thought. It was impossible, but God!

Mentoring: Being as much like Jesus as you can possibly be, so they can become as much like Jesus as they can possibly be

I would hold them accountable to high, often demanding standards. At the same time, I would show them deep, sincere affection and interest. It would be a balancing act. There had to be one deciding factor that would outweigh and trump every other element of our journey. I decided early on that it had to be the quality of my character. I would be on display and they would imitate me. I had to make a mentoring choice. I could show off my gifts or I could show off the character of Christ. Like most of us who have fought the good fight for any length of time, I knew that my gifts might get me started in the process, but only my character could keep me there. I had to look like, think like, act like, talk like and love like Jesus. Otherwise, the journey would be rough and the results not fully pleasing to the Lord.

When God calls you to the mentoring journey, take hold of your character and invest it with great care and caution. Christ-like character will return your investment with a bounty of fruitful works. However, if you lose your integrity in the eyes and hearts of your disciples, it cannot be regained. Your journey will be a fruitless trip through a wilderness of wasted time and effort. And God will not be pleased. You need to look like, think like, act like, talk like and love like Jesus. If you do, you will be like Jesus. That is ultimately, what He is after in the people He calls to mentor.

Invest your character with great care!

The Holy Spirit would have to be my Partner. I prayed that He would help me, anoint and enable me to be the best example I knew how to be. He answered me in a way I did not expect. It would be a singular and simple lesson I would apply to my young men, over and over, in our journey. Here is how it happened.

> One afternoon, I was in my office in our home in Suva. I was concentrating on my preparation for Sunday's sermon. I heard a call from the front gate. It was a group of my students from the School of Urban Missions. They had dropped by unannounced to visit us. They brought us a gift. It was a fresh, hot loaf of bread and some butter. (There is nothing this side of heaven that is better than fresh baked Fijian bread!) They had come, wanting to spend time socializing with Nancy and me. When I heard Nancy usher them into our house, my first reaction was to get irritated because of the interruption. I had just spent all morning teaching them. I had enough for one day. Besides, didn't they have assignments and evangelism to do? And I was really into writing this sermon. The revelation was flowing! I did not have time for this!
>
> I knew that Fijian cultural convention required that I go out and greet them. With my disgruntled, irritated attitude I did so. I left my desk and walked into the living room. There they were, with hands full of bread and smiles on their faces. They were so glad to see me. God is so good. I was crucified on the spot! My heart was immediately struck down because of my own callousness. Yet it was reborn in that instant with a whole new outlook. My season of blessing in Fiji really began right then in my living room. The Holy Spirit did more than just convict me of my sin, of my uncaring, unfeeling heart. That would be the

last time I put preparation for ministry ahead of the people of the ministry. That afternoon, God taught me to truly understand the value of the people he has given me to love and care for. Though my young warriors across the street were not with the students in my living room, they too, became the recipients of the moment. My newfound attitude toward these gift-bearing students became my attitude toward my guys living across the street. I would never be the same. I saw how priceless they all were to God. For the first time in my ministry, I truly saw how valuable the people God had given to me were. They were the essence of His blessings and grace in my life.

Understand the value of the people God gives you to love and care for!

What a moment that was! In that instant, I was *"filled with the knowledge of His will in all wisdom and spiritual understanding." (Colossians 1:9 NKJV)* God could now speak to me regarding what I could do, and more importantly, what I must be... as a man, a leader and mentor. I clearly saw the will of God was for me to engage my students and my young men with love. Nothing else would do! In that season in Fiji I learned the meaning of the Scriptural truth that, *"love never fails." (1 Corinthians 13:8b NKJV)* It is God's guarantee. The lesson was clear. I was to savor the time I would have with these young people with whom God had entrusted me. I took this lesson to heart and from that point on, I looked at my students and young men with very different, enlightened and understanding eyes. I served them the best I could in those days in Fiji - because the "eyes of my understanding" were now enlightened. (Ephesians 1:18 NKJV) I understood! I knew that my mentoring relationship with them would now be a relationship based on God's love. I knew this would please the Lord. In time, it certainly proved to please Nancy and me, as it did our students and our group of young warriors in the church. It was evident to the entire church. It became contagious. It ushered in the presence of God. We began to experience that rare time of revival when God mysteriously and marvelously touches His people.

It became obvious that my mentoring efforts and those of my associate pastor Emitai were bearing fruit. It was inviting and wholesome fruit, the kind that attracts people to taste of it. My group of young men were becoming like sons to me. They were growing and changing. They seemed to be walking in great integrity and faithfulness. They were gifted and unselfish in every way. I felt they were becoming so much like what I was trying to become for them. Their potential was being realized and I was encouraged. I was so proud of them! And then one day the unexpected happened. I had to call one of my young champions to come home to my office. It would not be a pleasant meeting. Expect the unexpected. It will surely happen!

Expect the unexpected. It will surely happen!

ꙮ Maika ꙮ

One of the brightest and most promising of my interns was Maika.[4] He had a quiet disposition. He was not the most prominent or vocal of the bunch. However, to a man, his peers held him in high respect. He was serious, intelligent and up until now, focused. He was on track for a bright career in ministry. Now he sat in my office about to face what

---

[4] The name has been changed.

could potentially destroy his hopes for a future in ministry. It had been discovered that he was breaking some non-negotiable rules that were required of all the church workers. It was an unexpected glitch in the program, his and mine. Now I would have to discipline him.

Maika sat down before me in my office. He knew he was in deep trouble. Church culture was not known to be easily forgiving in these circumstances. Others had suffered rejection in similar situations. I knew I could not let that happen. Yes, he would be held accountable, but I was determined to handle this mentoring challenge in a way that would become "a fruitful good work, fully pleasing to the Lord." The discipline I would impose on him would have to be proper. It would be uncompromising in its integrity and compassionate in its love. God was His judge, not me, but here I was, finding myself in a place where I could play God with his future. I would conduct the process of discipline, but discipline and punishment would not be what I was aiming for. My aim for Maika would be his complete restoration and a renewed conviction of his own integrity. The guiding principle in the disciplinary process would be that the experience would help him to increase in the knowledge of God, so that he would become more like Christ in character, word and deed. His failure would ultimately become a stepping-stone to his success. I knew that news traveled fast in the church. Everyone would be watching to see what I would do.

The Disciplinary Process

I cannot say I am an expert in disciplining people who have disappointed me in ministry. I do not think anyone ever becomes an expert in such matters. I am convinced there is no "one size fits all." Each person we face is unique. Their motivations, ambitions and personalities are different. However, we can develop universal principles of discipline that apply to anyone, anywhere. We will have to take these principles and shape our disciplinary and/or restorative practices to the person, context of the problem and the circumstances in which we find ourselves. I did this with Maika. I was not sure it would work until it did work. Most of the determining factors were out of my hands. They belonged to Maika and would manifest in his responses to the process and equally as much, to his relationship with me.

Here I was, faced with this unexpected, painfully difficult situation. Maika's future was in the balance. I needed a plan and I needed it quickly. What should I base my plan on? The answer was obvious. I would stick with the only things I could be sure of to guide and carry me through. So, I turned to the Word of God and the character of God. His Word and His character define Him for who He is. They are entirely dependable. They never fail us. I decided I would base the entire process of discipline and restoration on these two things. I would put a short leash on my own attitudes. I would judge the sin, and love the man. How could I fail if I took God's Word, added His character and filtered everything through His love? Together, they would take me through the process. They will always do the same for you.

Mentoring: The application of God's Word, the display of His character and the outworking of His love in you, instilling the same in others

The task at hand was difficult, but it would be no different that any other. I expressed my disappointment, and more importantly God's. I told him God cared deeply about him and so did I. My desire was to help him through this time. I would not abandon him. I asked him to search his heart and confess his sin to the Lord. I reminded him of Psalm 51, in which David cries out to God for forgiveness, a clean heart and a right spirit. I was careful with my choice of words. I condemned the sin, but not him. I knew he was in a delicate, emotional position. Nevertheless, this was the first step that would have to be taken. God's Word is very clear.

> *(1 John 1:9 NKJV) "If we confess our sins, He is faithful and just to forgive us our sins and to cleanse us from all unrighteousness."*

I asked Maika if he would agree to submit to my disciplining him. It was important to me that he understood, accepted and found value in my role in this process. There were consequences and they would be useful lessons in life. He would have to accept whatever I asked of him. I began to talk about what needed to be accomplished. I tried to do more than just lecture him on his failure. I spoke of opportunity in the midst of it. I drew him into the discussion and listened to what he had to say. We talked about his future as a minister and about his personal life. I reminded him of the seriousness of the call of God he had received, and the commitment involved in his devotion to God. It was a good beginning.

From there we talked about the primary goal of this disciplinary process. Whatever the goal was to be, it would have to fit into the four mentoring goals I previously set forth and committed to. Again, these were (1) a walk worthy of the Lord, (2) character fully pleasing to God, (3) efforts that would be fruitful and make a difference for His kingdom, and (4) a progressive increase in the knowledge of God and character of Christ. The goal of the disciplinary process would simply be for him to learn, grow and change - to be more like Jesus. This was nothing new, but it now had an urgent focus to it. It had to be a radical encounter with his own humanity at the feet of God's own deity! Only that would be life-changing!

How could we accomplish this goal? How could we turn Maika's failure into the kind of success that would cause him to learn, grow and change, so that his life would reflect more of the heart of Christ at work in him? Part of the plan was that as he progressed toward the goal, I would carefully and gradually restore him to ministry. When the time came for him to fully resume his ministry duties, I hoped he would be a different man, better for the experience and not likely to stumble again. I expressed my hope to him. The process of discipline and restoration would be painful, but it has been said, *"No pain, no gain."*[5] Maika could turn his failure into an opportunity for success. It would be more in his hands than mine. I was careful to encourage him and let him know I would coach him through the process. I was on his side. I was rooting for him to succeed and he knew it.

The goal of discipline: to learn, grow and change

So we walked together into the process of discipline and restoration. It was to be multifaceted. There would be penalties and requirements he would have to abide by. I would assign him tasks to perform, Bible studies, and written assignments to think through. We would spend regularly scheduled time in counseling. He would have changes in his lifestyle, and leave his comfort zones. He would have to pass the tests as they came upon him. In all this, I would be watching. It would take a great deal of my time. I was now judge, jury and parole officer.

[5] Source unknown

As for the penalties and requirements, they would begin with the denial of all ministry activities and opportunities until I was satisfied that he was making genuine progress. He was now on the shelf! He would have to move out from among our other young men. He would no longer enjoy the privileges of praying together with them daily or taking part in their morning devotionals and fellowship times. This may not sound as harsh as it might have been, but to him it was devastating. His lifestyle was wrapped up in his call to ministry. The young men he lived and worked with were like brothers to him. It was a strong rebuke he would have to abide by.

I imposed on him a heavy schedule of Bible study, having to do with sin, holiness and personal integrity. He would have written assignments that I designed to help him reflect on these issues. These would help us in our counseling sessions. (Ultimately, these were extremely fruitful, as we shared our thoughts openly and God moved faithfully in Maika's heart.) He would be required to continue to attend the weekly teachings I did for the leadership in the church. He would also be at all our weekly Tuesday and Thursday evening prayer meetings and would attend every church service. He would keep a journal of his feelings and thoughts. I would not read his journal. That was to be between him and God.

We did not establish a time-frame. I let him know that I would make the judgment on when to release and restore him to ministry. My criteria would be solely what I saw in him as the process progressed. I was asking him to submit to not just me as his pastor, but more importantly, to the leading and conviction of the Holy Spirit. I hope you can see the value and effectiveness of grace in all this. When you face similar situations, with all the accompanying anger and disappointment they bring, turn to God and cry *"Grace!"* He will give it to you.

Grace will turn a devastating circumstance into a teachable moment and a terrific victory!

Maika responded to all I asked of him. We agreed that he would begin one year of basic formal Bible school training. In time, he was fully restored to ministry. I was proud of how he turned things around. Even more, I was proud of who he became. I know the Lord was pleased.

That is not the end of the story. Something totally unexpected happened out of this situation. God not only turned this devastating circumstance into a victory for Maika, but He used another of my young men to show me I was on the right track with my commitment to them and was having some success in my mentoring. It came from an unexpected visit to the door of my office.

It was about two weeks after I placed Maika under discipline. I had gathered all of our young ministers in training and came down hard concerning the importance of integrity and honor among them. I left no doubt about who they would be letting down if they failed to maintain integrity. I would be disappointed, and that was important, but it would be God who really mattered. They were, after all, God's workers. My point was that their reverence for Him, coupled with their love relationship with Him should be so strong that they would not even consider letting Him down.

A few days later, another one of my interns came to see me. I sat him down opposite my desk and asked why he had come. To my surprise, tears began to stream down his face. I asked him what was wrong. As I said before, expect the unexpected. He had been deeply touched when I spoke to the guys about Maika's situation and told them I expected them to be men of integrity and honor. He had struggled within himself until now, and he decided to come and confess his transgression to me. What could it be to upset him so much? He told me what he had done. He was there to accept his punishment. I almost fell out of my chair.

It turned out that this particular transgression had happened several years ago, long before he came to be part of the ministry here in Suva. That was a relief of sorts! I asked him why he bothered to report himself, since it was so long ago and not connected to his ministry here. He was so convicted of his need to walk in holiness before God that he had to come to me to get it out of his system. I was amazed. It was the kind of moment that would melt the hardest heart. It was the beginning of a time in which we both would gain invaluable lessons that would help us to *"walk worthy of the Lord, fully pleasing Him, being fruitful in every good work and increasing in the knowledge of God." (Colossians 1:9-10 NKJV).*

I saw no choice but to place him under discipline and removed him from ministry for a season. He came through the process stronger and more committed than ever. He and Maika were two very different people, but my disciplinary/restoration programs worked themselves out in both of them. As with Maika, he required lots of my time, but the effort I expended with both of them was nothing compared to what it brought me. I came to understand even more, how valuable these two were to me. God seemed to be bringing that lesson home to me over and over. He desire to do the right thing would reinforce all the lessons I was learning with Maika. Their example would teach the rest of the boys what only these circumstances could teach. They opened my eyes even wider to the value and effectiveness of love in the mentoring process to which I had committed.

ꕥ Dan ꕥ

Dan was unique among my young men. He was a few years older than the others. His childhood and teenage years had been very difficult. He was probably not as educated as the rest. He was a tough guy who had been in trouble with the law in his youth. He spent a few years in prison (not a good experience in Fiji). On the outside, he was a big, muscular, intimidating looking man. On the inside, he was a teddy bear. For you to understand Dan, I have to tell you about an event in the life of the church.

> We had received the gift of a fine new keyboard from America. In Fiji, in order to plug in something electrical from America, it first must go through a transformer to reduce the voltage - or else you have instantly fried equipment. (American electrical equipment runs on 120 volts. In Fiji, the electricity is 240 volts.) We obtained a transformer for the keyboard, and I gave strict instructions that only the keyboard player or our worship leader was allowed to plug the keyboard in (for obvious reasons).
>
> One day, Dan, trying to be helpful, ignored my order and took it upon himself to plug in the keyboard. Dan did not know anything about electricity, except you plugged something in and it worked! He did not understand the need for the transformer, so he proceeded to try to plug our precious 120 volt keyboard directly into a 240 volt wall outlet. This was not

as easy as it would seem. Not only is the voltage different, but the prongs on the plugs are totally different. They could not possibly mate with one another, or so it seemed. That would not stop Dan. He decided to bend and twist the prongs of the keyboard plug to a 45 degree angle until they fit the slots in the wall receptacle. To this day I do not know how he did it, but he did! He literally forced them to fit the shape of the slots in the wall receptacle. He turned on the keyboard and yes indeed, it instantly fried itself! Shortly thereafter, I walked into the church. Everyone was standing around the keyboard just looking at it - well, everyone but Dan. He had climbed out the window and was crying on the ledge two stories up.

The keyboard was precious to us. It was a gift that had been sent nine thousand miles to fill a void in our worship. My first reaction was to blow my top. Somehow all the anger melted. I remembered that I was to treat my disciples with love. I did not feel much love at that moment, but grace immediately stopped me in my tracks! Grace touched my heart. Only grace could have melted my anger. After all, it was just a piece of equipment. Dan was not a piece of equipment! He was my gift from God. I would have to react so that I looked like, thought like, acted like, talked like and loved like Jesus.

I stuck my head out the window and asked him to come inside. I took him aside and put my arm around him. I told him that anyone can make a mistake and that the important thing is that we learn from our mistakes. I let him know that I was not angry with him and that I cared more about him than the keyboard. He was genuinely repentant and expressed to me that he would do whatever I required as his punishment. I did not punish him.

I embraced him. The power of grace in the mentoring process can be an amazing teaching tool. I learned grace over and over again in my time in Fiji. This was a divine appointment for both Dan and me. It was a teachable moment - not about keyboards, but once again, about what it means to journey together with people God has given you to love and care for.

Mentoring: Intentional Christ-like behavior for the explicit purpose of affecting others with His grace

These fine young men taught me that I cannot shape and mold anyone. It is a task only the Holy Spirit is up to. Submission to the process is every individual's choice. Ultimately, we all decide for ourselves what our lives become. My experiences with them confirmed for me the following:

1. The primary factor in my success as a mentor in Fiji was my attitude toward my disciples. How much would I value the opportunity to love and care for them, to nurture and help them to grow? My success would be directly proportional to the answer to this question.
2. If my life could model a richly positive walk with Christ, it would result in my disciples finding it worth emulating because I was found worth emulating.
3. My character, always on display as a mentor, would be more than a Christ-like example or personal trait. It would be who I am.
4. I would have an attitude of ever-increasing faith in God's ability to work within our imperfect human circumstances. My young charges would see it in me and catch it!
5. Daily, I would be identified as a faithful witness to Christ. I would refuse any other option in the ways I lived, loved and led!

6. It was never primarily about what they could learn to do, though I spent a great deal of time teaching them how to "do the work of the ministry." It was always about who they could learn to be. Who they became would be the true measure of our success or failure. We were in it together. I learned that even in the midst of circumstances of genuine human failure, a person can learn, grow, and become pleasing to God... and that defines true success!

   (2 Timothy 3:14 NKJV) "But you must continue in the things which you have learned and been assured of, knowing from whom you have learned them,"

What is Mentoring?

(From the definitions given in the pages of this chapter, above)

Mentoring is being as much like Jesus as you can possibly be, so they can become as much like Jesus as they can possibly be. It is done through the application of God's Word, the display of His character and the outworking of His love in you, instilling the same in others. This can be understood as the process of intentional Christ-like behavior for the explicit purpose of affecting others with His grace.

Chapter 3

They will Catch your Heart!

(The Value of Positive, Personal Affirmation)

ꕤ Jenny ꕤ

During our time in Fiji, one of our great joys was the opportunity to express God's love from our hearts to the people in our church. One of these was a young woman whose name was Jenny.[6] Looking back, I believe it was no coincidence that God put my wife Nancy and Jenny together. They were to have a divine encounter that would bring them each a special touch from God.

Jenny was a sweet college student. Our hearts would melt when she was around. She was introverted, insecure and exceptionally shy. She would hesitate to look you in the eye or carry on much of a conversation. She faithfully attended our church services and youth activities. She was obviously in love with Jesus. Jenny touched Nancy's heart. Every time Jenny walked into the church, Nancy would go toward the entrance to meet her. She would embrace her with a big, loving hug and give her a large, completely genuine smile. Every Sunday Nancy told Jenny how special she was to God and how glad she was that Jenny was there. This went on for the better part of two years until we finished our assignment in Fiji.

---

[6] The name has been changed.

Three years later we were invited by the CMF to return to the Fiji Islands for six weeks. We were to visit the churches our students had planted, renew old acquaintances and do a leadership seminar for their pastors. The CMF was gracious enough to provide us with a lovely home to stay in while we were there. It belonged to the personal advisor to the prime minister. He and his wife were living in government quarters while we were there, so we could be comfortable and get some rest between our commitments and activities, of which there were many each day. We found their home to be a blessing in unexpected ways. The living room became a place where visitors would come during the times we were not doing ministry. We welcomed them and sat for hours, reminiscing about all the good times we had in the past. Admittedly, we did not get much rest, but it was well worth it. One day there was a knock at the door. I answered it and there was a lovely young Fijian woman with a warm smile on her face. She radiated confidence and the love of the Lord was upon her. I did not recognize her until she said, *"I'm Jenny."* Well, I could hardly believe my eyes. What a transformation! Could this really be Jenny? What happened to the introverted, shy, insecure young woman who used to attend our church?

Here is the heartwarming, incredibly encouraging story Jenny told us. She said that she never forgot how Nancy met her every time she came into the church. She never said much to Nancy or anyone else about those times, but that day she told us how much she looked forward to Nancy's hugs and her words of loving encouragement. She listened to the things Nancy would tell her during those Sunday greetings. Throughout the rest of the week, she repeatedly spoke them to herself. In time, things changed. She began to believe in herself.

Jenny graduated from the University of the South Pacific and became a teacher. Her first assignment was to teach in what was generally regarded as the worst class in the worst school in Fiji. Her principal told her all she needed to do was baby-sit the kids and not worry too much about what they would learn. She was just to get through the year and she would get something better next year. The principal had no expectations for any significant progress or change in her pupils. Her reply to him was that she had every expectation that at the end of the year, her kids would be the best class in the school and even in the school system! He did not take her seriously. After all, she was new and had no experience in these matters.

Jenny continued with her story. What happened in the course of that year was too outlandish to be true, except that it was! The school year passed and the grades were counted. To everyone's surprise but Jenny's, her class not only had the best grades in the school, but scored among the tops in the nation. We asked her how she did it. She said that she never forgot what Nancy did and said to her in those greeting times in church. She was forever influenced by the warm, friendly hugs and all the affirmation she was given every time she showed up. She just tried to do the same with her students. Every morning, when the students came in, she would greet them with a barrage of genuine enthusiasm and love. She would tell them how well they were going to do and how great the year would be for them. She constantly affirmed them to be valuable and unique people, just as Nancy had affirmed her. The results proved that affirmation and love are a life-changing, winning combination. Jenny's students saw themselves in a different light. They saw themselves able to do what Jenny said they could do. That year their attitudes toward themselves and their futures changed forever. They became winners and champions, just like their teacher.

Jenny proved to herself, her students, and those around her that sincere, caring affirmation is foundational to the making of successful disciples. She actively pursued her dream of seeing her students catch what she caught from Nancy. She imitated Nancy who was simply doing her best to imitate Jesus. Jenny loved them unconditionally and her love did not fail. She helped her students to change their thinking about themselves and it transformed their lives. She proved that the very best God desired for those young people was not just possible, but would surely come to pass! What she accomplished was a picture of the grace of God in unstoppable, miraculous action! Jenny fulfilled her determination to make disciples who would find the same keys to success she had found. They had become like their teacher! Surely many of them continue today - fully determined to make a difference with those God gives them.

Mentoring: Helping people to transform their thinking so they can transform themselves into winners and champions

Jenny was a living, breathing example of Christ to her students. She shined brightly with the light of God's love. Her young people felt the warmth of the fire that burned within her. Even so, something had to happen in each of her students before they could burn with the same desire for the success they saw in her. And so, there was a quality needed within each of them that would carry them through. Like anything that will burn, they had to be combustible! They had to have something inside of them that would catch the fire that Jenny brought to the classroom. That would be their individual responsibilities and theirs alone!

When I reflect on what made the difference in Jenny, it was not anything Nancy did that was a deliberate effort to mold her young friend into somebody else. It was strictly Nancy's intentional display of genuine love for Jenny that touched her in such a way that it became the defining influence on the subsequent course of her life.

Mentoring: A process in which some things are taught, but other things must be caught

ꕥ Chialing ꕥ

(From Peasant to Princess)

Chialing was a lovely young woman. When Nancy and I first came to know her, she was extremely shy, soft spoken and insecure. She was very much like Jenny had been - a Cinderella who had not yet understood the favor she had from her King. She had graduated recently from a top university and was working as a therapist with babies and very young children who suffered from serious disabilities.

We immediately knew from observing Chialing in our worship services, that she was extremely sensitive to God, had a gift to worship and loved to be in church. She always came to our services with a smile on her face and a twinkle in her eye. She radiated her joy in the Lord. She would lose herself in the presence of God every time we entered into song in the worship part of the service. It was beautiful to see her do so.

She would often come to our house, and we would spend time with her, encouraging and affirming her. She struggled with low self-esteem and we were constantly reassuring her that she was somebody special, uniquely gifted by God, and could be all that God wanted her to be.

One day, much to our surprise, Chialing came to us and revealed that the Lord had given her a vision and desire to establish a weekly small group meeting for young, single women. It was in her heart but she was having a very difficult time getting it past her head... past her feelings of inadequacy. She knew her desire was God-given, but she had no confidence that she could do it. Yet, something compelled her to press ahead into this challenging, unfamiliar and uncomfortable ground. Nancy and I could see God's hand in it, and so we encouraged her. She had heard from God, it was to be her assignment. She would find a way to see it through. Of course, we were delighted to hear of it. We began to work with her to help her build her confidence and to ready herself for the task at hand.

It took a number of meetings, in which we did all we could to help her prepare for her first meeting. Though there was still much to do, a date was set. On her next trip to the house, she laid her plan out to us. It went something like this. For the first week, she had decided I would teach, and Nancy the next. Then she would ask our associate pastor to come and then... Well, we immediately made it clear to her it was not going to happen this way. We reminded her that God had clearly spoken to her and they were to be her meetings, not ours! It would be up to her to do the leading, teaching, praying and whatever else God required of her. Her reaction was not very far from panic, but she understood and agreed to lead them herself! Now that we were past this hurdle, the way was open for some serious mentoring! It was to be her time to let her light shine. She would have to step up and do all God asked of her. We knew she would do a great job. Now we prayed that she would see it and believe it too!

In the weeks that followed, Chialing came back to us and gradually unfolded the plan for her meetings. She had done a great job. She set up a schedule and assigned tasks to each young woman coming to the group. Everyone would contribute and participate. She began writing a Bible study lesson that we helped her to refine. We helped her to understand different creative teaching methods and to expand her ideas on how to conduct a Spirit-led group. Chialing was an excellent student and willing to allow the Holy Spirit room to guide her steps. Week by week she became more confident, and finally, it was time for her first meeting. Was it a great success? You bet it was! From then on, Chialing came to us every Friday afternoon with her plans for her weekly meeting. She continued to need our affirmation and guidance, but gradually, she grew into the role of teacher and leader.

Chialing's confidence level increased every week. She began to study the Book of Esther. She found a couple books on Esther that inspired her. She began to produce lesson plans and creative activities that revolved around Esther's life. Her relationships with those in the group solidified and became deeper, as did our relationship with her. As time passed, we knew it was her moment to take another step into leadership in the church. We asked her if she would occasionally do short weekly teachings on stewardship and giving in our Sunday celebration services, and to receive our weekly tithe and offerings. She accepted this new challenge and became very adept at relating to the congregation. God had given her a gift to take her life experiences and tell lovely stories that she then related to Biblical principles. The simple innocence in her stories had a profound impact when she told them. She quickly began to flourish in this new and potentially uncomfortable, public setting. She was now walking in greater assurance about her abilities to answer God's call.

(Esther 4:14b NKJV) "Yet who knows whether you have come to the kingdom for such a time as this."

Chialing found herself blessing others in ways that she never would have imagined. It became a great joy for her to stand and declare the goodness of God. She continues to step out in faith, stretching herself to explore new areas of ministry. She has truly walked in the favor of her King. Chialing now sees herself as a princess in His presence.

Mentoring: Involving our hearts with the hearts of those we mentor - In doing so, we encourage them to reach for their dreams and embrace their destinies.

Both of these young women, Jenny and Chialing have shown us the diversity of God's ways with our disciples. They were each unique, but also very much alike. Jenny's mentoring experience was very different from Chialing's. Jenny was influenced by simple, sincere and compassionate expressions of Nancy's love. It was never our intention to commit to mentoring Jenny. We never made overt efforts to engage her in the mentoring process. On the other hand, with Chialing, we recognized what God wanted to do in and through her, and we determined to help press her into the mold God had prepared. This was intentional mentoring on our part. It was consistent and constant effort. It was not always easy and could be downright exasperating. However, she did make the trip and it was a glorious one!

Through these two young women, Nancy and I learned and reaffirmed some important lessons about mentoring and life. When God gives us people to love and care for, to mentor and encourage, we must recognize and distinguish the differences between them. Each will be precious and unique. Each will have a distinctive call on their lives. We will influence every one of them best by the genuine, Christ-like love we show them, and by the wisdom we use in how we try to influence them. For some of them, we will simply be who we are in Christ to them. Others will need more active mentoring efforts. Then there will be some who will need to be shaped and molded by our consistent, deliberate and often demanding efforts. Any way it happens, it will be by the grace and power of an interested, committed and loving God.

Both Jenny and Chialing lived their Cinderella stories. Each found their way to the palace on their own distinctive paths. Their stories remind us that mentoring is not simply a collection of skills. It is the manifestation of God-given relationships in which people catch our hearts and hopefully some of our wisdom! What is most important for us to remember is that we must focus on their personal growth, not their personal usefulness to us. We are to be careful that our perceptions of how they might serve the kingdom of God do not cause us to manipulate their lives.

Focus on their growth, not their usefulness!

Jenny and Chialing have favor with God. They are His princesses. He is their King. They need not wait for an invitation. They are always welcome to come near. He put it in their hearts to dream of palaces. The same is true for those princesses He gives you. He will always be more interested in what they can become than how they might be used! Always remember, God loves them more than you ever could. Rest in that fact and be encouraged. Know that when they catch your heart, they will grow into their destinies.

(Esther 5:1-3 NKJV) "Now it happened on the third day that Esther put on her royal robes and stood in the inner court of the king's palace, across from the king's house, while the king sat on his royal throne in the royal house, facing the entrance of the house. {2} So it was, when the king saw Queen Esther standing in the court, that she found favor in his sight, and the king held out to Esther the golden scepter that was in his hand. Then Esther went near and touched the top of the scepter. {3} And the king said to her, "What do you wish, Queen Esther" What is your request? It shall be given to you; up to half the kingdom!""

The Heart of a Mentor

I have often wondered how the people I mentored perceived what was in my heart. If they were asked to describe what my heart contained, if they were to diagram it, how would they label its characteristic parts? I know what I desired my heart to be like. My desire was that it would always be a good model for others. I asked them to catch what's in it!

If mine is the heart of a typical mentor, and I modeled or diagramed it as a puzzle with all its pieces, what would it look like? How many pieces would there be? What would each piece be labeled? Would some be bigger than others, or would they all be the same size? Would there be room for unlabeled pieces, for new growth? Let me suggest a few labels I consider vital for the heart of a mentor.

A Grateful Heart

It seems to be the human condition that we are seldom as aware or appreciative of God's favor and goodness as we ought to be. It has always been so easy to take what God had blessed me with for granted. Too often I have been unhappy because of what might have been, could have been or should have been. It has been easy to lose focus on God and forget that I walked in His favor.

When our commitment in Fiji was complete, it was time to give the church and school of ministry to our replacements, and head back to America. I looked ahead to enjoying the things we used to take for granted in America. I began to think about what it would feel like to buy a good car instead of having to take the broken down taxis and exhaust-spewing busses that we used every day in Fiji. I looked ahead to the unlimited variety of foods available in the American supermarkets. But what about leaving the people we loved so much? What about the blessings of living among them, and, the miracles we were privileged to be a part of? Would I ever have another opportunity like Fiji gave us to train so many warriors for Christ?

The day came when we officially turned the church and school over to others. In the weeks following, we saw firsthand, the heartfelt loss our people were suffering. We had to let go, and found our own hearts painfully empty. Our people had brought so much joy to us. We understood how incredible a gift the season in Fiji was. When we left Suva for the airport, most of the church accompanied us and blessed us with more gifts than we could carry home. I practically had to stuff Nancy in a suitcase to bring her back to America. I think if they could have fit, half our church would have been in there with her!

We always have so much for which to be grateful. Most of all, we can be grateful for the people God gives us to watch over. They will be acutely aware of, and sensitive to the ways we display our feelings. Knowing this has forced me to limit the time I allot myself for personal pity parties (which have always been far too frequent for someone who should know better). Knowing they are watching has also helped me to get rid of my unjustified irritation toward others (which also has been far to frequent for someone who should know better). I ought to be grateful for them instead. These good people, who have been so appreciative of me, have kept me on my toes and motivated me to check my attitudes. Think about it. Isn't it easier to be grateful in a crowd of other grateful people.

> *(Psalms 103:2-5 NKJV) "Bless the LORD, O my soul, And forget not all His benefits: {3} Who forgives all your iniquities, Who heals all your diseases, {4} Who redeems your life from destruction, Who crowns you with lovingkindness and tender mercies, {5} Who satisfies your mouth with good things, So that your youth is renewed like the eagle's"*

> *(Psalms 105:1, 3-5 NKJV) "Oh, give thanks to the LORD! Call upon His name; Make known His deeds among the peoples! {2} Sing to Him, sing psalms to Him; Talk of all His wondrous works! {3} Glory in His holy name; Let the hearts of those rejoice who seek the LORD... {5} Remember His marvelous works which He has done, His wonders, and the judgments of His mouth,"*

We ought to be wearing the words of these two Psalms like familiar, well used T-shirts. Being grateful is much easier when we remind ourselves of what the Lord has done.

A Compassionate Heart

To be compassionate means to have a *"sympathetic consciousness of others' distress together with a desire to alleviate it."*[7] We must be careful not to confuse compassion with pity. To have pity on someone implies *"tender or sometimes slightly contemptuous sorrow for one in misery or distress."*[8] Pity does not necessarily include a desire to do anything about the misery and distress. So, there is a world of difference between the two. Pity is simply a feeling, an awareness of someone's trouble. Compassion is so much more. It begins with a feeling, but is coupled with a determination to do something about what we feel. God expects us to have hearts of compassion, not pity.

In my early years of ministry in America I was mentored by a gifted pastor. At the time he was Pastor of Single Adults in our church. We had about a hundred people attending our single adult services. It was there I learned the basics of ministry. I began with the simplest tasks, such as setting up the sanctuary for every service. I learned to set up and tear down the sound equipment. I was taught how to usher. I was included in countless counseling sessions. I was stretched by the preaching and teaching opportunities my pastor gave me. One thing he taught me well was how to pray for people. I very quickly became very good at the mechanics of public ministry. I could preach, give an altar call and pray for people - one after another with hardly a sweat!

My mentor had a great influence on many people. His was an exceedingly fruitful ministry. Yet, in the midst of it, my heart never caught his compassion! In time my mentor moved on and I was given his ministry. I became the Single Adult Pastor. Many things changed,

---

[7] Merriam-Webster's Collegiate Dictionary, Tenth Edition, ©2000, Springfield, P.234.
[8] Merriam-Webster, P.885.

but my praying was like ice fishing! I was cold and numb toward those I prayed for. I functioned well and appeared to be doing the job, but I had no compassion. My prayers were empty and deficient. There was no life or love in them.

One Friday night, I was preparing for the evening's service. I was in a corner of the altar, praying. I distinctly heard a voice within me say, *"Do not pray for anyone until you feel the compassion I feel. Make yourself ready. I will honor it."* It was a moment that defies explanation. It was an intensely personal encounter. From that time until this, I have never prayed for anyone without checking my heart and being sure it was filled with compassion. I must admit, there are still times when I stand before someone for what seems like far too long. I will only pray when I have found the compassion. I have spoken of this many times to those I mentored. Sometimes they catch it and sometimes it goes right past them.

We are to imitate the heart of Christ, who did not pity us, but had compassion for us. He is our example. We are to have compassion on those without Christ. We are to have compassion on those who are hurting, sick, disadvantaged and downtrodden. Remember, those we care for and those we mentor will catch what is in our hearts. Let them catch the compassion!

> *(Matthew 14:14 NKJV) "And when Jesus went out He saw a great multitude; and He was moved with compassion for them, and healed their sick."*

> *(Matthew 25:35-40 NKJV) "'for I was hungry and you gave Me food; I was thirsty and you gave Me drink; I was a stranger and you took Me in; {36} 'I was naked and you clothed Me; I was*

sick and you visited Me; I was in prison and you came to Me.' {37} Then the righteous will answer Him, saying, 'Lord, when did we see You hungry and feed You, or thirsty and give You drink? {38} When did we see You a stranger and take You in, or naked and clothe You? {39} Or when did we see You sick, or in prison, and come to You?' {40} And the King will answer and say to them, 'Assuredly, I say to you, inasmuch as you did it to one of the least of these My brethren, you did it to Me.'"

An Understanding Heart

There are two shades of meaning for this word, "understanding." To have understanding is, first of all, to comprehend or have a grasp of what really confronts us. Second, it means, *"to show a sympathetic or tolerant attitude toward something."*[9] When we combine both of these shades of meaning they work together to bring us wisdom. Understanding is a safety net God gives us as leaders. It prevents us from falling into error and enables us to make good decisions about those we lead.

The Bible tells us that God appeared to King Solomon in a dream, and asked the new king, *"What shall I give you?"* Solomon's response is illuminating to the mentoring process. He knew the value of understanding.

(1 Kings 3:7-9 NKJV) "Now, O LORD my God, You have made Your servant king instead of my father David, but I am a little child; I do not know how to go out or come in. {8} And Your servant is in the midst of Your people whom You have chosen, a great people, too numerous to be numbered or counted. {9}

[9] Merriam-Webster, P.1284.

therefore ***give to Your servant an understanding heart to judge Your people****, that I may discern between good and evil. For who is able to judge this great people of Yours?""*

Solomon later recorded this proverb concerning a man with an understanding heart. It is wisdom for the ages!

(Proverbs 1:2-5 NKJV) "To know wisdom and instruction, To perceive the words of understanding, {3} To receive the instruction of wisdom, Justice, judgment, and equity; {4} To give prudence to the simple, To the young man knowledge and discretion; {5} A wise man will hear and increase learning, And a man of understanding will attain wise counsel,"

In those times when I face tough decisions, I often think about my young disciples sitting in my office admitting their transgressions. I remind myself of the patience and understanding it took to formulate my response to their situations. I had to respond to more than the act of sin. I had to respond to them as people. I had to understand them with my heart, not just my head. Only then could I give them the godly correction, instruction and wise counsel they needed. Understanding has a way of taking us beyond ourselves and giving us a glimpse of how God sees things.

Learn to show a heart of understanding to those God gives into your care and you will never go wrong! You will find the wisdom that comes from above and it will help you to make right decisions and take right actions. You will mentor without becoming a tormentor. You will lead and guide your followers fruitfully. They will be blessed with good success.

A Steadfast Heart

Steadfastness is an attitude. It is formed out of the raw material of our character. It is displayed by our actions. It lives in our hearts. To be steadfast means to be, *"firmly fixed"* on a course until completion; *"not subject to change"*; and *"firm in belief, determination or adherence."*[10] Its opposite is to be indecisive and noncommittal. To be steadfast is to be faithfully committed to the course of action until we reach the finish line. Steadfastness causes us to abound or thrive in the work of the Lord. We persevere by the knowledge that God is with us and that our course is right and pleasing to Him. We know it will have eternal significance. This knowledge gives us courage to face the challenges, tests and trials every one of us will have in our service to God. A mentor's finest prayer for his disciples and himself is that we all persevere until the end.

> *(1 Corinthians 15:57-58 NKJV) "But thanks be to God, who gives us the victory through our Lord Jesus Christ. {58} Therefore, my beloved brethren, be steadfast, immovable, always abounding in the work of the Lord, knowing that your labor is not in vain in the Lord."*

> *(Psalms 57:7 NKJV) "My heart is steadfast, O God, my heart is steadfast; I will sing and give praise."*

> *(Psalms 112:7 NKJV) "He will not be afraid of evil tidings; His heart is steadfast, trusting in the LORD."*

---

[10] Merriam-Webster, P.1146.

A Diligent Heart

Diligence is the twin brother of steadfastness. They go hand in hand. Diligence is defined as "*steady, earnest and energetic effort.*"[11] Its opposite is lazy and apathetic disregard for the task at hand. In our diligence, we fix our hearts firmly on the course we are given, taking the initiative to act faithfully, no matter how long it takes or what we might face. When we reach the end, our hearts have been steadfast and the will of God has been accomplished! Results: Those we mentor are well equipped for their futures. We get the victory. God gets the glory!

> *(Proverbs 12:24 NKJV) "The hand of the diligent will rule, But the lazy man will be put to forced labor."*

It has been said, *"Quitters never win and winners never quit."*[12] The spiritual weapons we have been given to fight the good fight of faith will gain us eventual victory in our trials and tests. Our spiritual armor is complete. Nothing is lacking. We have what it takes to win our battles decisively. We can be steadfast and diligent to the end. God assures us in His Word that we are able to finish the fight of faith and still stand! A steadfast, diligent heart is the heart of a finisher!

> *(Ephesians 6:13 NKJV) "Therefore take up the whole armor of God, that you may be able to withstand in the evil day, and having done all, to stand.*

I remember how much some of our ministry students in Fiji struggled. The curriculum I had designed was challenging. They were not used to English as a first language, and they had to adjust to my western ways of teaching. It was intimidating for them. It was apparent to me they

---

[11] Merriam-Webster, P.324.
[12] Source unknown

were in over their heads. I had to make significant adjustments in the ways I taught them. With great patience I determined to look beyond the norms and standards I was used to applying to my students. There were learning curves they could not yet navigate. There were cultural chasms I would have to help them cross so that they could reach the potential awaiting them on the other side. I knew they could make it. I just had to be as diligent as they were and guide them with an unfailing heart. It was an incredible stretch for all of us. They would not quit, nor would I. We persisted together. The timing and circumstances were different for every one of them, but eventually understanding and revelation came to them all. In those moments each passed beyond their personal walls of difficulty and intimidation. The result was a group of men and women who were standing in their victories. They truly believed they could do anything God asked. Together, our diligence and steadfastness made a way for them to move confidently ahead, knowing they would be fruitful in the work of the Lord.

A Merciful and Grace-filled Heart

God does not call mentors to be drill sergeants. Having once been a U.S. Marine recruit, I can attest to the fact that there is little mercy or grace programmed into a drill sergeant. Their task is to remove the recruit from everything familiar and to tear the recruit down emotionally until there is a blank slate to work from. Then, using a variety of motivational tools, including a heavy dose of fear (and certainly with a lack of compassion), the recruit is remolded to think like his mentors. Unfortunately, this is sometimes the way we deal with our recruits in ministry.

God's ways are not like those of a military drill sergeant. God is a loving Mentor. His methods are always instructive and encouraging.

Jesus is our mentoring Model. He was relational with His disciples. He loved them and taught them by the words He spoke and the life He lived. He prayed for them and He prayed with them. He looked at them through a lens of mercy and grace. They were His friends. They were imperfect but He looked past their imperfections. They were weak, but He gave them strength in their weaknesses. They were not always faithful, but He showed His faithfulness in spite of their faithlessness.

(Ephesians 2:4-5 NKJV) "But God, who is rich in mercy, because of His great love with which He loved us, {5} even when we were dead in trespasses, made us alive together with Christ (by grace you have been saved),"

A Loving Heart

(1 John 4:7-9, 11-12 NKJV) "Beloved, let us love one another, for love is of God; and everyone who loves is born of God and knows God. {8} He who does not love does not know God, for God is love. {9} In this the love of God was manifested toward us, that God has sent His only begotten Son into the world, that we might live through Him... {11} Beloved, if God so loved us, we also ought to love one another. {12} No one has seen God at any time. If we love one another, God abides in us, and His love has been perfected in us... {16} ...God is love, and he who abides in love abides in God, and God in him."

1 John 4 gives us some hard lessons about love. The Apostle John leaves us without excuse, argument or compromise. He reminds us that God paid the highest price for His love toward us - the death of His

Son Jesus. The message is that God is as serious about love as He can be. John tells us "*everyone who loves is born of God and knows God.*" It is clear that if we cannot label love as a significant element of our hearts, it is a sure sign we do not know God. John says that the person who "*abides in love abides in God and God in Him.*" To abide is to rest comfortably and permanently in one place - a place we can call home. When we abide in the love of God, we have settled there with our friends, chief of whom is God. Once again, it comes back to relationships! Love is the master key to our relationships with God and with those we mentor and care for. There may be other considerations which are significant and even essential to these relationships; but only one, the love of God, is its master key. As you know, a master key opens every lock, and therefore every door. Love removes every barrier. It never fails. It reigns eternally.

Mentor your people with the love of God in your heart. It will never fail you… and if you keep it before you in your mentoring efforts, you will never fail God. I had to invest many things in all those wonderful people. My relationship with each of them was unique. Some of the circumstances and many of the ways I approached those relationships were also unique to each one. Yet, one thing remained the same for every relationship and every mentoring effort. It was God's insistence that I abide in love toward each of them, just as He did. Love became the key that opened the doors to success for us all. Trust your mentoring to love. It will never fail you.

A Holy and Uncompromising Heart

The heart of a mentor is not only under God's watchful eyes, but under our own. To be holy and uncompromising refers to the character of God, made available in us. It is not referring to the question of legalism or rules. It concerns itself with the issues of the heart. We have God's Word and we have God's Spirit to lead and guide us. He will instruct and convict us of everything that does not please Him. We must love what He loves and give no place to what He has no place for - the issues of sin.

Here again are the basics of what they will catch from our hearts. These are the eight pieces or characteristics of the heart puzzle we have just discussed.

1. Grateful
2. Compassionate
3. Understanding
4. Steadfast
5. Diligent
6. Merciful and Grace-filled
7. Loving
8. Holy and Uncompromising

Of course, this is not a complete list, but it goes a long way toward defining the heart of a mentor. There is so much more inside of us that God wants to bring to the people we mentor. If you were to grade yourself on these eight pieces of the heart puzzle, what kind of grades would you give yourself?

In Chapter 2, we referred to Colossians 1:9-10, in which we find the Apostle Paul's prayer for his Colossian friends. Look at it again. This is my prayer for you and for those who will catch your heart.

> *(Colossians 1:9-10 NKJV) "For this reason we also, since the day we heard it, do not cease to pray for you, and to ask that you may be filled with the knowledge of His will in all wisdom*

> *and spiritual understanding; {10} that you may walk worthy of the Lord, fully pleasing Him, being fruitful in every good work and increasing in the knowledge of God;"*

Can we describe the intent of our hearts as, *"fully pleasing to the Lord?"* We know that we are still imperfect human beings. Not everything in our hearts will please Him. We also know, thankfully, that He has the grace to look beyond those things. We are all works in progress. If the people you mentor catch your heart and your intent is to be *"fully pleasing to the Lord,"* then you will be the source of influence God wants you to be.

What is Mentoring?

(From the definitions given in the pages of this chapter, above)

Mentoring is the act of preparing others for life's tough decisions. It is equipping them to be ready for the inevitable choices they will face. Mentoring is involving our hearts with the hearts of those we mentor. In doing so, we encourage them to reach for their dreams and embrace their destinies.

Chapter 4

It takes a Father to Make a Son

(The Value of Positive, Personal Affirmation)

(1 Timothy 1:2a NKJV) "To Timothy, a true son in the faith."
(2 Timothy 1:2a NKJV) "To Timothy, a beloved son"
(Titus 1:4a NKJV) "To Titus, a true son in our common faith"

ꕥ Naca ꕥ

(Pronounced Na-tha)

A True and Beloved Son in the Faith

There comes a special time in every mentor's life when God sends a singularly exceptional person to be mentored. My special time began out of my experience with one of our young ministers in training in the Fijian church. His name is Naca. From the day I met him, I was aware he possessed exceptionally strong faith, talent and zeal. He was a gifted dancer and worshiper. He had raw preaching gifts I knew would develop into something special. He was a born youth evangelist, with an almost pied-piper affect on children and young people. That was good, but it gets even better. What impressed me most about Naca was his truly humble and serving heart. He was almost too good to be true… but he was!

As I have written earlier, our young workers were established in a good training routine. They were settled into a house that had been lent to the church for them to live in. It was just across the street from Nancy and me. I was pleased with their response to me and the system we had in place. Most of their supervision was being carried out quite efficiently by my assistant pastor, Emitai, who lived with them. He saw to their needs and assigned them their daily tasks. I was therefore able to concentrate on those things that were important to me for mentoring the group. Then the day came when we lost the use of the house they lived in. I met with the elders of the church and we decided we would split everyone up and have them live among the elders. Naca came to live with us.

Naca moved into the spare bedroom next to the office I kept in our home. He became very special to Nancy and me. We grew to love him as a son and he loved us as a second set of parents. He was easy to love, even though we had to overcome some definite cultural differences. Nancy and I still laugh about how he had to be asked not to use her hairbrush, and how Nancy had to get used to him using her dish cloths as handkerchiefs. We always found we could work around the cultural issues and thanked God for him. He was a wonderful gift to us. Naca was one of the brightest, most gifted people we had ever met. He was full of faith and exuded the joy of the Lord. He was contagious with compassion and mercy. He had a great smile that drew people to him like a magnet!

Naca had given up more than most to serve the Lord. In addition to the daily hardships that came with his life of faith as a church worker, he suffered through barriers that would have stopped many from accepting the call to serve. Naca came from a poverty stricken family. He had been raised in the public housing projects of Suva. We learned that, in spite of his circumstances, he had been given a scholarship to the finest private boy's high school in Fiji. He had been "first boy," or tops in his class, but upon graduation he walked away from a scholarship to the University of the South Pacific. He did so in answer to God's call, and began serving full-time, as a worker in the church. We learned that his parents had thrown him out of the house and refused to communicate with him for many months because of his decision to walk away from the university and serve the Lord as a full-time worker. His dedication to God was beyond question. He was fully committed to his calling and the unfolding course of his life.

I could write volumes about Naca's faith and the exemplary life he led when he lived with us in Fiji. He was everything we could ask him to be. However, if I were to major on what he did, and what he became in Fiji, it would not drive home the point I want to make about him. The extraordinary story of Naca revolves around who he was, and who he remains to this day. To understand this, I have to take you from 1996, when we met him in Fiji, to 2001, half a world away in New York City. There Nancy and I discovered how much of a son he had become to us. Here is how it happened.

In November of 1998, when our commitment in Fiji had been completed, Nancy and I felt God calling us back to America. The church and the School of Urban Missions were given into the hands of two men who were handpicked by Pastor Suliasi Kurulo, president of the Christian Mission Fellowship, whom we had served. And so we left Fiji to return to America, to our home church and to await new marching instructions from the Lord.

In less than a month's time God spoke to us. We felt the Lord leading us to New York City. Talk about totally different mission fields! We responded with great anticipation and hope. We arrived in New York City in February 1999 and planted an international church on

Roosevelt Island. We began the work through relationships we established with people in the United Nations. Our newly growing church primarily consisted of families from the diplomatic service, mostly from the nations of the South Pacific, including Fiji. We found ourselves with a number of children and teenagers. They had been taken out of their Pacific Islander cultural contexts and thrust into a very different New York City scene. We needed someone who could relate to our young people as our children's and youth pastor. We had no doubt it could be Naca. We contacted Pastor Kurulo and requested that Naca be released from his ministry there and allowed to come to New York City for a three-year period. As he ministered in our church, he could be further mentored and equipped in so many ways. Then, when he went back to Fiji, he would be a great asset to the work there. Pastor Kurulo agreed. After obtaining the necessary immigration clearance, we awaited Naca, who would shortly be on an airplane headed for America. It looked like all our plans would fall into place nicely, but as I wrote earlier, expect the unexpected!

A Ride on a Runaway Freight Train

(My Suffering, Naca's Disappointment… Our Ultimate Victory)

Just three weeks before Naca was scheduled to arrive, I went to the doctor for a routine physical. I was long over-do for a checkup. When the doctor received my test results the following week, he immediately sent me to an urologist. The first thing the urologist said to me was, *"You have prostate cancer. You have had it a long time. It's like a runaway freight train heading downhill and it's likely going to kill you!"* As I heard those words, the gift of faith rose up inside of me, *"I don't think so."* We entered a season of walking in faith like we had never experienced before. Into this unexpected situation came Naca. He arrived with great anticipation that he would be working in an exciting environment, doing what he could only have dreamed of in the past. He would be a youth pastor in New York City. It was a long way from the public housing projects in Fiji.

Naca arrived at John F. Kennedy Airport in New York City on a very cold day in November. I will never forget the look on his face when he walked out into the icy blast of cold air. It was a new experience for someone who had enjoyed the warmth of the balmy South Pacific. We all laugh about it to this day. What we don't laugh about is the turn of events that stopped me from pastoring our new church and dashed all our expectations. As things progressed, I was sent to receive radiation to combat the disease. It was a rigorous and difficult time. I was weakened greatly by the treatments, and experienced some unusual side effects. I was so stricken that within a month's time I could no longer function in ministry. I would spend the next five months in serious pain, unable to do much except struggle to get ready to face the radiation machine and then come home to lie back down. We had no choice but to close the church, as I could no longer pastor. All of our efforts and energy would now be to get through this trying time. Here was Naca, finding his own dreams seemingly dashed along with ours. He saw the church he had come to serve closing its doors shortly after his arrival. It would be, for all of us, a time of great trial and testing. His would be a very different New York experience than he expected.

In a very real sense, Naca became our source of encouragement and joy during his time with us in New York City. I was fighting my way through my bout with cancer, unable to do much for myself because of the complications I was experiencing. When Nancy was just too tired to care for me any longer, Naca would step in and do whatever was necessary. I remember a number of occasions when I would be laying on our sofa in great discomfort and Nancy would massage my feet.

When she got tired, Naca would just step in and take over for her until I got past the fog of pain and fell asleep. At other times, he would pick up his guitar and sing or just play softly until I got through a particularly trying moment.

Naca would get up every day at four o'clock in the morning to pray and intercede for me. (Although Nancy finally had to ask him to put his alarm under his pillow, as the alarm was loud enough to awaken us in the next room. We love to pray, but four in the morning was a bit much for me under the circumstances.) He was always willing, doing whatever helped and never complaining. He was more like a son to me than if he had my blood flowing through his veins. All three of us thought his coming to New York City would be the fulfillment of our dreams and we would build a great church together. God brought him to us for very different reasons.

Mentoring: An experience in which disappointment and denial can become open doors to new dreams and the fulfillment of God's best

Living with Naca through the experience of my illness taught me a great deal about him. He was the same person I first knew as one of my young disciples in Fiji. His habits had not changed. His gifts remained the same. He still had to be reminded not to use somebody else's hairbrush or blow his nose into one of Nancy's dish towels. But those things held no importance as we experienced the character of Christ demonstrated in this young Fijian man.

Could it have been that God sent Naca to us so that his presence and powerful prayers would be there in the midst of my struggles? I know that God cared so much about all three of us that he planned ahead to put us together in my time of greatest need. It was the favor of God in action! God was glorified in my suffering, in Naca's disappointment and in our ultimate victory. Our experiences together changed us forever. We drew closer to God and to each other. We understood more than ever before, what it meant to trust God in the midst of the trials and tests of life. In time, what was very bad would result in what was very good. All of our disappointments, mine, Nancy's and Naca's, became an opportunity for another appointment - an appointment with God! All things truly do work together for good to those who love God. If you are experiencing disappointment today, make an appointment with God. He will have much to say to you.

Remember, disappointment is an opportunity for another appointment - an appointment with God!

(Romans 8:28-29a NKJV) "And we know that all things work together for good to those who love God, to those who are the called according to His purpose. {29} For whom He foreknew, He also predestined to be conformed to the image of His Son..."

The day came when I walked out of the doctor's office, and walked into my future. I was walking in the results of nothing less than a series of miracles. I had my divine healing. Now God would take us out of the ashes of our battle to the light of a brand new day. I understood more fully the meaning of beauty for ashes and a garment of praise for a spirit of heaviness. As for Naca, he would soon know firsthand, another chapter in the favor of God for his life. He would have the joy of seeing the Lord's plan come to pass for him. God would once again show Naca that He was totally trustworthy and gracious. We were on our way to Florida.

We arrived in Florida, back at our home church. At the time, the church had about two thousand people. Naca was invited to become an intern in the youth ministry. For the next two years, he would be mentored by some incredibly competent and creative youth ministers. He would be given great ministry opportunities in a very strategic youth ministry. He would have experiences he never could have had in New York City. God rewarded him fully for his unwavering faith in Him and faithfulness to us. He would have an extraordinary opportunity to prepare himself for the next season of his life and ministry. It would be a time he would never forget.

Time passed swiftly. Naca's three-year visa was coming to its end. We discussed whether or not he should get an extension and stay another three years. Pastor Kurulo had graciously released him from the Christian Mission Fellowship for three years, so that he could be trained and equipped, and then sent back to Fiji. He was expecting his return. The temptation was there for him to turn his back on this obligation and extend his stay in America. In my role as his mentor and spiritual father, I helped him walk through this issue. He decided what was right and did it. He would continue in the perfect plan and will of God. He would honor Pastor Kurulo and go back to Fiji.

I watched as Naca struggled with the decision, but I never doubted he would do the right thing. It was his obedience that opened new doors for him upon his return to Fiji. When he arrived, he was able to establish a national youth ministry. He was given entrance into every school in the country, to preach the Gospel and bring his message about abstinence and character to the nation's young people. He established a ministry to homeless teenagers and adults. Doors opened up for him to preach in many places. He was given an opportunity to do a weekly radio program for youth. It became the most popular program in the country. He married and God moved him into new opportunities. He and his wife Laisa continued his ministry and added their presence to a ministry to homeless and abused women and their children. Nothing much changed about Naca's character and commitment, except that it grew even stronger. He remained faithful and fully committed to the Lord. What more could a mentor ask of a disciple? What more could a father ask of a son?

Mentoring: A process that focuses on character and commitment - All else we teach rises or falls, succeeds or fails, on these two issues.

As I began to write this book, Naca was one of the people I asked to contribute a paragraph or two so his perspective on the mentoring experience could speak for itself. Below is part of what he sent me. English is his second language and I quoted his response exactly as he wrote it.

"My name is Nathanieli... I grew up in the projects but my parents were still so broke they couldn't even afford a $5 a week rent let alone put 3 square meals on the table for us. To come home to a pot of tuna fish stew is a rare luxury. With 5 children and 2 adults in a one room apartment, no place to study, no TV and radio, life I can say was really tough. The one room served as our kitchen, dining room, living and bed room.

The new Pastors of the church were an American couple known as the Abramsons. Bob and Nancy Abramson. They came and being the only white people in the church then, the locals were kind of shy and timid around them at first. As time went on, we warmed up to them and thus began a beautiful and healthy relationship between the church and them. They brought with them what many in the church back then and still today refer to as "madrai katakata" or "hot bread." It was fresh from Heaven. No one will ever forget Nancy's teachings on Sunday morning. It is still referred to today. Many, in asking a brother or a sister how they were doing would add to that question the phrase "Would you like me to sit in the mud with you"? which was from one of her Sunday morning teachings. At the time of the change over, the church's bank balance was so far down the red end that we've forgotten what orange looked like. Anyway, when Pastor Bob came, he didn't tell people to give their money or do fundraising. He came and he taught the Word. As the Word was taught, the people's hearts were moved and many as a result of this gained a new understanding of what Kingdom living really is. Many began to realize that the Lord doesn't want them to owe any man anything, which at that point in time was the life story of a lot of the church members. The church within a few months became debt free and many doors were opened and people began seeing breakthrough after breakthrough in their lives. Many still do to this day.

The church began growing and in 2 years, the church grew from 60 to around 350 people…it could be more but that was how phenomenal it was. We began having prayer meetings twice a week on Tuesdays and Thursdays from 5pm – 8pm. We also opened up the church for lunch hour prayers from 12pm – 2pm and they came by the hundreds. We not only had awesome prayer meetings, but our worship service was incredible. For the first time, many of the church members had heavenly visitations. We were in the middle of a full blown revival. We were part of it and to us it became a normal part of our lives but for those who came from outside, they could tell that something was unique about the place. God was in the house.

The Abramsons somehow by divine inspiration or just pure love for a mother/fatherless young worker took me under their wings. They took me into their home and loved me like I was their own child. Not only was I loved and treated with respect, they gave me my own room. Up until this time, I had never had my own room. It made me feel really special for the first time in my life. I didn't know what I did to deserve all these but as I got to know them better, it occurred to me that they were not merely interested in my enjoyment and comfort. They were interested in something greater. They wanted me to understand what it means to live here on with an eternal perspective. They helped me to realize that a man can walk through life on a daily basis in sweet communion with the Lord. All this time, I thought that my whole purpose in life was to set up chairs, clean the toilets and teach Sunday school. All that is well and good but that's not where God wanted me to pitch my tent. He wants me to go higher and deeper in the things of the Spirit. He wants me to be fully aware of what's going on in the spiritual realm because only then can I fully understand the natural and how it affects our lives.

Through all this, I continued to grow personally. One other thing that they helped me to take a hold of was hearing the voice of the Lord. Being around the Abramsons birthed in me an awareness of the ever present presence of the Lord. I became sensitive to the Holy Spirit's leading as a result of this. It was this training and impartation not as from a teacher to a student but from a father and mother to their son which has helped me to make some major decisions in my life.

Finally, I would like to thank my parents in the Lord, the authors of this book, Dr. Bob and Nancy Abramson. Dad and mom, what else can say? There really isn't enough words to express how eternally grateful I am for you. You have taught me how to live as a man. You've taught how to love, how to pray and how to hear that still small voice and I still do. I am the man I am today because God blessed me with the two of you. Whenever I am down, you encouraged me to encourage others who are down. Whenever I need help financially, you taught to sow into those who need finance. When I am lonely, you taught me to find strength and joy in the Lord. By teaching me those life principles, you've taught me everything. Now, I can boldly say that I will be successful in life because God was gracious enough to bless me with you two to guide and train me in my younger days. Thank you so much. I am so looking forward to that day when we will be able to minister together again. Until then, my prayer for you is that you will be in health and prosper even as your souls prosper. Moce mada sota tale." (In English - "Good by and see you soon.")"

Show them the heart of God. Teach the principles of His Word. You will teach them all they need to know.

Mentoring does not mean Duplicating Ourselves

(1 Corinthians 11:1 NKJV) "Imitate me, just as I also imitate Christ."

In an earlier chapter, we explored the question, "What is mentoring?" It is easy to make the mistake of planning our efforts around a wrong understanding of the process. Mentoring is not the process of duplicating ourselves in our disciples. To imitate is not to duplicate or replicate. It is not to make a copy of an original. To try to do so would be fruitless and frustrating. Mentoring is the process of instilling a desire for imitation in your disciples - imitation of someone far greater than you! The Apostle Paul never said, *duplicate me just as I duplicate Christ.* It is not possible to duplicate ourselves, and certainly impossible to duplicate Christ. There is a fundamental difference between duplication and imitation. If we could duplicate ourselves, it would be no better than cloning - stamping out an exact copy. To attempt this would be to deny the divinity of God and the uniqueness of His creation. Instead, we are called to imitate or reproduce the character and qualities of Christ in ourselves and to model them for others.

Mentoring: A commitment to the act of coaching, in which we point the way for others to imitate and embrace the same lifestyle we are trying our best to imitate and embrace - the lifestyle of Christ

Our goal should be that our disciples see and value the characteristics of Christ at work in our lives. Then, they will be drawn to imitate us. When this happens, God will do what only He can do to reproduce the faithful sons and daughters He is after.

Mentoring is the process of instilling a desire for imitation of someone far greater than you!

ꕥ Emitai ꕥ

I met Emitai the first day of our new ministry training school, the School of Urban Missions, in Fiji. He was one among thirteen of the Christian Mission Fellowship's most promising young men and women. They had been given into my hands for a year. I was to equip them to take the Gospel to the cities of the nations. At the completion of their studies, my students would be eligible for ordination and would be sent out to their new assignments. Some, including Emitai, had already been on the mission field and were recalled to attend our school. Emitai had led a team of missionary evangelists to the interior of Papua New Guinea. He had been through dangers and hardships most of us only read about. In the first days of school, he sat there, said very little, as he tried to absorb the teaching. As the weeks and months progressed, I became seriously impressed with his work ethic and his obvious leadership skills. I was now convinced he was somebody with extraordinary potential. He was single minded about the Gospel. He was the complete package… and God was speaking to me about him. There would be destiny in our relationship.

Look for the destiny in them and you will find the destiny in yourself.

Emitai and the Crocs

Every Thursday evening, Nancy and I would have the students over to our home for fellowship. We ate together and then we all sat around on the floor of our living room. (Nancy will never forget the time that the students managed to make fourteen sandwiches from one small can of tuna fish.) There were always a couple people who brought guitars. We sang songs and told stories. The students recounted their times on the mission field. Nancy and I soon learned that in Fiji, a funny story retold over and over is just as hilarious as the first time, if not more so. We found ourselves laughing hysterically over stories we had heard a dozen times, even though we knew ahead of time what the punch line would be. The stories of their missionary exploits were fascinating. Sometimes they were more sobering than funny. These times gave us great respect for our students and a sense of humility at being there to mentor them. For me, one of these stories stands out above the rest. It was about Emitai's previous missionary travels to Papua New Guinea. It goes something like this.

> Emitai was leading a team of seven young evangelists into the mountains and primitive backwaters of Papua New Guinea. They went by faith. They had little or no money. They were on foot, carrying Bibles, gifts and other items necessary to the task. As they were traveling, they encountered a river. At its edge was a man with a small boat, which he used to ferry people across the river for a price. It would require two trips to get across - one for Emitai and his seven team members and another for their supplies. Emitai approached the man and asked how much it would cost to be taken to the other side. The man gave him the figure and Emitai knew that they only had enough money between them for one trip to the other side. The

crossing seemed problematic. Emitai thought about the situation. They were short of money, yet, they had to get across. He gathered his team together and said, *"We are going to put the supplies in the boat and pay the man for one trip across. Then we are going to swim!"* That is what they did. They made it to the other side, picked up their equipment and continued on their way.

One of the students asked Emitai, *"Wasn't that dangerous? Weren't there crocodiles in that river?" "Oh yes,"* Emitai replied. *"So we prayed and believed God for our safety, and we swam across... but you know what? We swam across real fast!"* Of course, the students had heard this story a hundred times. Each time it was repeated, someone would ask Emitai that same question about the danger of the crocs. He would always reply with the same answer, and we would laugh hysterically every time he said, *"We swam across real fast!"* Nancy and I joined in the laughter, but we also knew the sobering truth this story demonstrated. Each time we heard it, we were reminded of what kind of warrior for Christ we had been entrusted with to mentor.

(Mark 9:23 NKJV) "Jesus said to him, "If you can believe, all things are possible to him who believes.""

Mentoring is like a swim in deep waters. When the waters get deep and seem dangerous... pray, believe God and keep swimming! You will make it to the other side.

One Small Favor

The year passed and it came time for our inaugural class to graduate. This was an important milestone for the Christian Mission Fellowship and for the students as individuals. In the year they had spent with me God did incredible things in all of us. Though I had taught in Bible schools in America and New Zealand, it was in this inaugural classroom that I learned how to teach with the Holy Spirit as my Partner. Now my thirteen spiritual sons and daughters would be leaving and going to their next assignments in the islands of the South Pacific and even across the globe. I had been aware of a still, small voice for some time, urging me to pursue the potential in Emitai. I went to Pastor Kurulo, the head of the Christian Mission Fellowship. We had great respect and admiration for each other. We both saw the school as having an excellent and successful beginning. The international church I pastored was flourishing. I felt confident in approaching him and in the way of Fijian respect, I quietly asked him for *one small favor*. I asked for Emitai! Well, specifically, I asked if Emitai could be my assistant pastor in the coming year.

I knew I was to continue to work with Emitai and speak into his life. He was like a diamond in the rough and I wanted to keep chipping away at the edges. I knew he was extremely well suited to all that the position of assistant pastor in our church would demand. Even more than that, I knew he was destined to fulfill his purpose - to be an influential senior pastor-evangelist on the mission field. He would have great fruitfulness. I wanted to stretch him and challenge him on a much more personal and intense mentoring level than I could the previous year. I planned for him to live with and direct the activities of our young men (Naca included), who were full-time workers in our church. He would join with our church elders under my tutelage and would have plenty of opportunity to learn the principles and practical things I wanted to impart to him about church leadership.

Pastor Kurulo said yes to my request. I was there when he called Emitai into his office and gave him the news. I wish I had a camera to record the expression on Emitai's face. He was blown away! To continue with me was something most of the students had been hoping and praying for, but it was Emitai who God answered. He could hardly believe it had happened. He was beside himself. So was I.

We got on with our year together in the CMF International Church. Emitai fit in and functioned like a glove on the hand of God. He was loved, respected and looked up to by our people. He moved in with our workers just across the street from our home, organized their lives and pretty much cracked the whip when it came to keeping them busy. They began each morning with a long run in the predawn darkness, proceeded to prayers and devotions among themselves and went from there. They ate together, prayed together, worked together and learned together. Emitai was a master at this. They idolized him and had no small degree of fearful respect for him. They responded willingly to his mentoring and in a military fashion to his demands. I was amazed at how he got things done. He was personally disciplined and demanding of himself. His young charges saw this and caught on. They became highly organized and disciplined in their spiritual lives and work ethic. It was good for us all. I taught him, he taught them... and they all taught me. Emitai matured into exactly what God had programmed for him to become.

I knew this young man was an extraordinary asset for the kingdom and the work of the Lord. His ways were different than mine. They were not wrong. They were very right! In fact, anyone introduced as a missionary into the uniqueness of a new cultural context must gain an understanding of this truth. I knew there would be limitations to my perceptions of what he was doing. There is always a cultural bridge of understanding that we can never completely cross. Yet, there is value on each side of the bridge that needs to be embraced by those on the other side. I saw the wisdom in giving Emitai room to do things in his Fijian way. He saw the value in catching my heart and learning what I wanted to impart to him. The experience helped us both to see the value in diversity, and grow in our abilities to minister across cultures. It was a season of expansion, joy and satisfaction for everyone concerned.

Give them room to be who they are. Keep your mind as open as you have kept your heart.

Mentoring: A process in which we give our disciples room to be themselves, freedom to do things their way and opportunities to discover the value of our ways

Some of my fondest memories of Emitai are the times he would show up at our house just in time for breakfast or lunch. Nancy would typically make him a plate of eggs (lots of eggs!), bread and butter, and beans. Emitai would eat as much as we could put before him. It was something to behold. I still think of him, sitting at our table with his plate emptied, a satisfied look on his face, muttering, *"Beans!"* How he loved those canned beans! He never tired of them. Needless to say, we never tired of him. He was in many ways, very much like Naca. He too, was a son to us. We loved and respected him.

The day finally came when Emitai's year as our assistant pastor was finished. He was reassigned by Pastor Kurulo to plant a church on the other side of the island. In a short time, he had a growing, faith-filled church that was a reflection of all that was in him. He pastored in his own, unique way, but many of the things he learned or caught from me were now part of him and his ministry. At this writing, he, his wife and their three children are back in Papua New Guinea, where he pastors a large, growing church and conducts a great outreach into that country.

> *(John 15:14-16 NKJV) "You are My friends if you do whatever I command you. {15} "No longer do I call you servants, for a servant does not know what his master is doing; but I have called you friends, for all things that I heard from My Father I have made known to you. {16} You did not choose Me, but I chose you and appointed you that you should go and bear fruit, and that your fruit should remain, that whatever you ask the Father in My name He may give you. {17} These things I command you, that you love one another."*

A Spiritual Father's Commitment

- I will be sold out to my calling as a spiritual father - to the point of absolute reliability.
- I will remain fully convinced of the rightness of the path of spiritual fatherhood I have chosen.
- I will be grounded in the character and purposes of God, at work in and around me.
- I will give my best and always believe the best in those I am committed to.
- I will trust God, knowing that my disciples are always and ultimately in His hands.

- Above all, I will strive to be the kind of spiritual father whose motivations and actions are consistently found to be well pleasing to God!

(2 Corinthians 5:9 NKJV) "Therefore we make it our aim, whether present or absent, to be well pleasing to Him."

Put all these principles together and become a practitioner of excellence with them. You will be a living epistle, demonstrating the love of God, the heart of God and the hand of God at work through you. To be a father involves so much more than planting a seed that begins a life. A father is defined by his commitment. He is proven by his willingness to stay the course until the time of release comes. Then he lets go and allows his sons and daughters to become all God has destined them to be. Even after their release, a father's commitment continues. The ties between spiritual fathers and their sons and daughters always ought to grow stronger. The commitment of a spiritual father is unique in its power to influence. It is a blessing from the Lord.

The Gift of Spiritual Grandchildren

ꕥ Sakiusa ꕥ

It was the year following my recovery from cancer. We had left New York City and gone back to Florida with Naca. I had been away from Fiji for almost three years. I received an invitation to return and spend about six weeks ministering there. One of the high points of the trip would be a whirlwind journey around Fiji visiting the graduates of the School of Urban Missions who had planted new churches. One of them was Sakiusa (everyone at our school called him "Saki."). He had planted a church in the mountains of Northern Viti Levu[13] in a village community of gold mine workers.

We arrived at the village in time for an evening service. Saki was in tears just to see us again. After the people of the church had gathered, Nancy and I were ushered out to the yard behind Saki's house. He had erected a series of poles made from trees which held a canopy of corrugated iron. There were no sides to this structure but it served as a very nice church. Electric lights hanging from bare wires illuminated the area. At the front was a pulpit constructed from some rough looking wood. Behind the pulpit sat two overstuffed chairs that had been brought out from the house for Nancy and me to sit in. Perhaps seventy-five people had gathered, and were sitting on mats on the ground awaiting our arrival. They were all new converts that Saki had won to the Lord. They were ready for church.

After the congregation had worshiped and prayed, Saki introduced us. It took him about twenty minutes to tell the congregation how much we had meant to him, and how his time with us had changed him forever. He finally turned to Nancy and me, sitting in our overstuffed chairs. The few words He spoke to us carried more impact than all he could have said had he stood there for hours on end. The words he spoke will ring in my heart forever. He simply said,

"Pastor Bob and Sister Nancy, I want to introduce you to your spiritual grandchildren."

When you find you have spiritual grandchildren, they will be the evidence you have done what God asked of you. You have fulfilled your task to make disciples who themselves become disciple makers.

[13] Viti Levu is the Fijian island on which Suva is located.

In that church of gold mine workers, I saw seventy-five people who were born again, sincerely thankful. They were imitating Pastor Saki, just as he had imitated me, and as I imitated Christ.

From what we have said, we can establish these four principles of Biblical mentoring:

1. Mentoring is based on imitation. It is not reproducing yourself in someone else.
2. Imitation is an exercise of free will. It cannot be forced.
3. Your disciples will imitate whoever you imitate, good or bad.
4. The character and heart of Christ is to be clearly and consistently imitated and modeled by the mentor.

> *(Matthew 5:16 NKJV) "Let your light so shine before men, that they may see your good works and glorify your Father in heaven."*

What is Mentoring?

(From the definitions given in the pages of this chapter, above)

Mentoring is the father-like process of building character and commitment. It is an experience in which disappointments can open doors to new dreams and the fulfillment of God's best. Teach them to expect the unexpected, and welcome it.

Mentoring is the act of coaching, in which we point the way for others to imitate and embrace the same lifestyle we have imitated and embraced - not ours, but the lifestyle of Christ. In this process we give our disciples room to be themselves, freedom to do things their way and opportunities to discover the value of our ways.

Chapter 5

Landmarks in Their Lives

A landmark is a clearly recognizable sign of a significant historical event, or an achievement worth noting, taking place at a particular point in time. I have often thought about the landmarks my disciples will place along the paths of their lives. Have you ever considered what you should be able to see in your disciples, long after they have gone on beyond the times when you actively influenced them? What will their lives say?

Mentoring happens in very different ways. It may occur in a classroom setting, a one-on-one situation, or in those times when people are simply affected by our presence and example in leadership and life. Our mentoring experiences will be colored by two characteristics which work together. These are, first and foremost, the quality and depth of the relationships we have with the people we mentor, and second, the effects of the circumstances we walk through together with them. I love to get reports from places I have never visited where my disciples now labor. I love to hear about the landmarks they are establishing with their lives. Think about the people you have discipled. Can you look back on some of the validating signs or landmarks that help you see the measure of their successes? These landmarks will give you a window into the measure of your time spent with them, and help you to know you have done the job well.

I want to touch on five key landmarks that have proven to be good indicators of the fruitfulness of my own mentoring experiences. I believe you will find them equally useful in looking strategically at your own efforts. These indicators are valid in any cultural context or situation.

1. Continuing Fruitfulness after they have left you
2. Reports of their Steadfast Character and Christ-likeness
3. Genuine Humility in the Conduct of their Lives
4. Indisputable Signs of the Lordship of Christ
5. Compelling, Unwavering Service to God

Each of these five landmarks will give you insight into the purposes and goals of the Christian mentoring processes you are committed to. As we go through them, I hope they will both inspire you, and help you structure your unique, particular assignments as a mentor. Let's examine them one at a time.

First Landmark: Continuing Fruitfulness after they have left you

(John 15:8 NKJV) "By this My Father is glorified, that you bear much fruit; so you will be My disciples."

(John 15:16 NKJV) "You did not choose Me, but I chose you and appointed you that you should go and bear fruit, and that your fruit should remain, that whatever you ask the Father in My name He may give you."

ಬಿಣ Netani ಬಿಣ

About half way through our time in Fiji, Nancy and I moved to an apartment at the edge of a cliff, overlooking the harbor in Suva. We did so primarily because it was close to downtown and we could walk to school or church. The place had a picture-postcard view from our living room windows. You could see all the ships in the harbor and the mountains beyond, which made a beautiful backdrop. Outside our windows was a porch. It was about four feet wide and hung over the cliff, with a drop of about four hundred feet. When Nancy went out on the porch to hang the wash out to dry, she had to be very careful of her own safety. If she ever dropped an article of clothing, it was history.

We rented the apartment for the view and regretted it from the first day. When we first inspected the apartment, we neglected to notice the road far below that carried in excess of a hundred busses an hour in and out of the city. When we moved in, we quickly learned that toxic vehicle exhaust rises. We also neglected to notice the noisy all-night taxi stand directly across from our front door, or the fact that the busy national hospital was just next to it. It was there that I again experienced what the Apostle Paul meant when he wrote, *"all things work together for good to those who love God and are called according to His purposes" (Romans 8:28 NKJV).*

Immediately below us lived a woman named Diana, who had come to know the Lord and was attending our church. She, her six children, and her mother were living in a two-bedroom apartment. Netani, the husband and father, had left Fiji to study and was living out of the country. She was doing her best to raise their six children. She had extremely limited financial resources and could barely keep bread on the table. When Netani returned home, Diana insisted that he come to church every Sunday. He did. As the weeks went by, we could hear the arguments going on below us. Invariably, Diana would come upstairs to share Netani's latest escapade. In spite of his various misadventures, he honored his word and kept coming to church. He would sit there every Sunday morning with his arms stiffly folded, with his countenance in no uncertain terms revealing his displeasure at being there. Needless to say, as the pastor, I was not the most popular person in his life. If you ask Netani today about that time, he would say he hated me.

On one particular Sunday, a friend of mine from America, Pastor Chester Clarke, was preaching a week of revival meetings for us at the church. Right in the middle of his sermon, the power of God hit Netani. He suddenly found himself being thrust backward out of his chair onto the floor. He just laid there and shook. We did not consider this terribly unusual. After all, we were a fully charismatic church in a developing nation, where the unusual was commonplace on any given Sunday. Netani lay shaking on the floor until well after the service was finished. I was a bit surprised at how long he lay there, but did not give the incident too much attention. What I did not realize at the time was that when he got up and stopped shaking, he would never be the same. His was the classic case of a Damascus Road experience. He had met God and God knocked him off that chair. He did not get up until God was through dealing with him. When he finally got off the floor, he was a man who had received a visitation and now had a revelation of Christ. Old things had passed away and all things had become new (2 Corinthians 5:17).

Over the next months, I marveled at the changes in Netani. He was being transformed. His behavior radically changed. It was a complete reversal. He began to demonstrate the qualities of a God-fearing man, a terrific husband and a loving father. He worked hard and in time, was successful in resurrecting his business, which had shut down in his absence. (He was a trained architect and contractor.) It became clear to all of us in the church that the fire of God now burned in his heart. It seemed to grow hotter by the day. He poured himself into the Word of God and soon became an integral part of our church life. He felt a call to serve me and began to look for any way he could do so. When I would go to an outlying village or town to preach, he would take the day off and drive me there. He would even fly with me when I had to go to another island, just so he could sit and pray for me as I preached. The fire inside of him grew stronger and stronger. The experiences we had together convinced me God was in the process of doing something unusual. To my amazement, we went from our bad beginnings, in which he hated me, to the unlikely place where he was becoming my faithful friend. Even more, I soon recognized God had given me a willing disciple, a man who could say with great conviction and thanksgiving that he had once been lost, but now had found his way. God was speaking to him and calling him to a path he never would have imagined. Together, he and I were fast becoming deeply involved in his amazing transformation.

Whenever Netani accompanied me to another church, where I was to preach, I would ask him to share a few words on stewardship just before the church received their offerings. It did not take him long to become comfortable with this. There was simplicity about his words and it touched the hearts of his listeners. This gave him valuable exposure to speaking in front of a congregation. He had a speaking gift and I was able to help him begin to develop it. He and his wife Diana became leaders of a strong fellowship group in their home. His natural gifts for leadership were surfacing. As time went by, I brought him into the inner circle of our church leadership. He easily bonded with the other men whom I relied upon to partner with me in the leadership functions of the church.

The day finally came when I really pressed him with a challenge. I asked him to become one of my church elders. He was floored that I would even ask him. I knew this was to be my next step in mentoring him. It would be both a great challenge and a great affirmation that old things had truly passed away and he was on his path to his purpose and destiny. He knew I would hold him to high standards and would not tolerate any reversals in his behavior. I told him so very clearly. He rose to the challenge and was an excellent elder. Within a year after I left Fiji, Netani could no longer deny the call of God. He enrolled in the School of Urban Missions. Upon completion of his Bible school education, he went on to earn an M.B.A. from the University of the South Pacific. His business continued to flourish. He had become a pillar in the church.

Challenge them to respond. They will go places in God only He could make possible.

Finally, Netani felt God calling him to a season of change, a season with great potential. He migrated to Canada with his family, which had now grown to eight children. He believed God would establish his ministry there and his children could have a better future. He is now building a successful life there. At this writing, he has been ordained a minister of the Gospel and found his place on the staff of a great church in Vancouver. He is active in missions work back to his native Fiji. He has plans to enroll in a course of study leading to a Ph.D. in Intercultural Ministry. He believes it will help him reach across the cultural boundaries that have separated God's people and become an effective missionary back to his nation.

Netani is writing a success story with his life, his family (now nine children) and his ministry. We often communicate with each other, and remain friends to this day. He continues to ask my advice and relies on my counsel. I have watched him walk with God, with his steps surrendered to the Lord. He is an example of the potential every one of us has to journey through those landmarks of success and significance that await us, if we will surrender to the revelation of the lordship of Christ.

Long after people have ceased to be under your direct influence, you will get reports they have been light to their worlds. Their great, sometimes unexpected, and even surprising stories of success will signal that you gave them what God asked and it stuck! As you can see, my story of Netani is a great example and I hope it inspires you as it does me. His light continues to shine and people around him continue to glow with it, and they grow ever closer to Jesus. If your disciples continue beyond their season with you, displaying their personal growth and fruitfulness, then you will have done well.

This first landmark, Continuing Fruitfulness after they have left you, will confirm that your mentoring efforts were correctly designed and effectively applied. Your influence produced people whose dedication and efforts will continue to multiply the Kingdom. You blessed the people God chose for you and your fruit will remain.

Second Landmark: Reports of their Steadfast Character and Christ-likeness

Mentoring is an identity and character forming process. It produces people who look like, act like, talk like, walk like, think like and love like Jesus. Expect those you touch to mark their journeys in life with their steadfast character and Christ-likeness. Look for reports that repeatedly affirm that the power of God has miraculously changed them. From time to time, word will come to you that they have kept what you gave to them and are using it well. They will show the world around them that they have been transformed into the image of Christ. They now display His character. They can be depended upon to be like Him. They can be expected to achieve the potential God placed within them and empower others to be like Jesus. They will be fruitful for His kingdom.

> *(2 Timothy 2:15 God's Word Translation) "Do your best to present yourself to God as a tried-and-true worker who isn't ashamed to teach the word of truth correctly."*

If you do your best, you can be confident they will do theirs. They will influence others with the character and selflessness you showed them. You will have accomplished your assignment. Netani's example has built my confidence. If you ask his family and friends… if you ask his current pastor… if you ask his ministry contemporaries, and if you ask those he presently ministers to, they will tell you his life has made theirs richer and taken them closer to God. I have done my part, so Netani can do his. It just feels so good!

If you do your best, they will do theirs.

I am determined that I will do what is necessary to bring about positive personal growth in my disciples. I want to know that those they minister to, both now and in the future, will have the same opportunity to be changed, as they had. Our primary mentoring purpose (which is God's singular Biblically stated purpose), is that all who follow in the continuing chain of mentorship become more like Him. I have been overwhelmed by the goodness of God, as I watched the changes occur in those He gave me, and later heard of their faithfulness, long after we had parted. These reports have made my struggles and sacrifices worth more than all the riches I might have acquired, had I traveled any other path. I want to promise you, your heart will fill with gladness when you look back and count the many who now look like, act like, talk like, walk like, think like and love like Jesus, because you cared enough to do the same.

> *(Romans 8:28-29 NKJV) "And we know that all things work together for good to those who love God, to those who are the called according to His purpose. {29} For whom He foreknew, He also predestined to be conformed to the image of His Son, that He might be the firstborn among many brethren."*

Mentoring: Doing your best to insure they will embrace and fulfill their destinies

Third Landmark: Genuine Humility in the Conduct of their Lives

This may come as a surprise to you, but genuine humility can neither be taught, nor can it be caught. Let me explain. Genuine humility is not a learned behavior. Neither is it a tangible set of principles we put into action, nor a particular body of knowledge we hold within us. Though you and I may have it, and understand how it works, we cannot teach it to anyone. It is not waiting somewhere out there to be apprehended. We cannot let down our nets and catch it, like so many fish in the sea. The only way genuine humility comes is when *it catches us!* In a moment of time, it apprehends us. We surrender to it and we are undone! Imagine the humility that flooded Thomas when Jesus asked him to place his hand in the Lord's wounds. All Thomas could do was to cry out, *"My Lord and my God!" (John 20:28 NKJV)*

My friends and I have often joked about giving each other an award for being the most humble. Such a thing would be an absolute contradiction. I think God anticipated this, when He designed humility to be something only He can get credit for. In that special moment when genuine humility catches us, we recognize that God is God and we are not! Genuine humility, therefore, can be understood as an outward expression that follows an inward encounter with the Holy Spirit. He moves on us and we are caught. We are captured by the reality of the cross of Christ! We realize the magnitude of what God has granted us. He has given us what we never deserved and held back what we did. We are humbled in the face of His holiness and grace. It is a response from within our spirits. It changes our souls. I can best define genuine humility to you in this way. It is a spiritual response to an understanding of self, in light of a revelation of Christ.

Genuine humility is a spiritual response to an understanding of self, in light of Christ.

I invite you to ask yourself if there is pride working inside those places in you that nobody sees? Be honest with yourself. What will you find?

Take a moment to reflect on this challenge. Now ask yourself, how often have those hidden things found their way to the surface anyway, so everybody could see them? I will admit to you that I am not smart enough to keep them hidden. My guess is that you aren't either. Pride is smarter than either of us! However, when you and I stay surrendered to humility, pride cannot hide itself, nor have its way for long.

Pride is hard to kill. It is dangerous, eagerly waiting to devour us if we let it usurp the place of humility in our hearts. Give pride an inch and it will take a mile! Give it no place and it will have no place.

> *(Philippians 2:3, 5-8 NKJV) "Let nothing be done through selfish ambition or conceit, but in lowliness of mind let each esteem others better than himself...{5} Let this mind be in you which was also in Christ Jesus, {6} who, being in the form of God, did not consider it robbery to be equal with God, {7} but made Himself of no reputation, taking the form of a bondservant, and coming in the likeness of men. {8} And being found in appearance as a man, He humbled Himself and became obedient to the point of death, even the death of the cross."*
>
> The International Children's Bible says it this way.
>
> *"...do not let selfishness or pride be your guide.... {7} He gave up his place with God and made himself nothing... {8} And when he was living as a man, he humbled himself and was fully obedient to God. He obeyed even when that caused his death--death on a cross."*[14]

[14] Portions of Philippians 2: 1, 7-8

I can only testify of my own struggles with pride, for who can really look within another? Revelation from within has not always been easy on me. It required me to make new, sometimes tough choices, and to rethink ones I had previously made. It required me to reject what my flesh wanted to treasure. Often, I discovered that some aspect of my thinking or behavior I previously looked at as treasure was really nothing but trash. What an empowering change this discovery brings! In Chapter 3, I shared one such moment with you. It was when I was praying prior to an evening service, and the Lord spoke these words to me, *"I love them. Do not pray for them until you have found it in your heart to love them too."* Genuine humility caught me. The Holy Spirit showed me how He really saw them, and it humbled me. I was found out. I was apprehended and even shamed. I began to see the people I was about to pray for in a different light. Since that moment, I have resolved never to pray for anyone without taking time to find the compassion and humility I should have.

I have watched similar times of inward revelation and change become landmarks in the lives of Netani and others, as pride was replaced with humility. My guess is that you will agree such times have been equally key to you.

Sometimes I wish it were easier to remember that Christ is God and we are not. Genuine humility can be a struggle. That is the way of fallen humanity. Each struggle has the potential to be a life-changing event. Teach this to those you mentor, so they will anticipate, recognize and accept it when it comes. In such times, we are challenged to serve the Most High with an even greater resolve. Just as Paul did when he was humbled before the Lord on the road to Damascus, all each of us can ask is, *"Lord, what do you want me to do?" (Acts 9:6 NKJV)* I pray that you and I will continue to ask that question with humility in our hearts. We can be sure He will respond, and we will have our marching orders. Let me encourage you. Demonstrate humility in all that you do. Your disciples will do the same. You will watch them identify ever more closely with what it means to be like Christ. They will become a living picture of the grace of God. Others will see the grace, and be caught as they were. Genuine humility paves the road to our destinies. I cannot explain it, but Jesus will travel that road with us, and meet us when we get there.

Fourth Landmark: Indisputable Signs of the Lordship of Christ

ജ Daniel ജ

In Chapters 2 and 4, I introduced you to Emitai, my associate pastor in Fiji. One day he came to me and asked if I would accompany him on a visit to a business office in town. There was someone there he wanted me to meet. We went to a small storefront on one of the main streets in downtown Suva. I was introduced to the owners who then showed us the way to a small office, where we found Daniel.[15] He was sitting at a desk, reading his Bible. Daniel and Emitai had first met somewhere on the streets of Suva. I cannot recall where, but the important thing was that Emitai led him to the Lord. This was only the beginning. Emitai visited him in the office a couple times a week. He began to build a relationship with him and disciple him. Daniel was more than willing. He was eager to hear all Emitai had to say. When Emitai led him to Jesus, Daniel had his road to Damascus encounter. He was hungry for all he could know. Emitai had invited him to bring his wife and family to church, but he felt it important to introduce me personally to Daniel.

[15] The name has been changed.

So there I was, face to face with this unassuming new convert, who was about to tell me his story. I did not know it at the time but it would be the beginning of a God-ordained relationship between us. It would be an experience that conquered my tendency to make quick judgments of what I saw in people. As a result, our relationship would teach me not to put limitations on what I expected because of what I thought I saw in others (a lesson I seem to need reminding of every now and then). Here is Daniel's story.

Daniel had been trained as a stockbroker and investment counselor. He was brilliant, but had, for some time, applied his brilliance to a career of dishonesty. Word travels fast in a small nation like Fiji, and his reputation was a national ruin. Everyone knew of the various schemes he had worked. He had defrauded a large number of people. It was common knowledge he could not be trusted. He, his wife and their children were destitute because nobody would trust him enough to employ him. The people who owned the business where we met had compassionately and graciously given him a small salary just to answer the phone and be in the office when they went out. He told me he had been arrested for his dishonesty and was out on bond. He faced thirty-two counts of fraud, and was scheduled to go to trial shortly. As I sat across from him that day, I listened politely and tried to be an encouragement to him. However, I held no great expectations for his future. It looked like it was too late. He was sure to be locked up and out of my life soon. I had seen others like him who said the right things because they were facing jail.

The very next Sunday, Daniel brought his family to church. Over the weeks that followed, He and his wife joined in the life of the church. They were there every time the doors opened. Daniel could be found with the men of the church, praying and praising at every opportunity.

The family became part of our small group ministry. In the midst of all this, Emitai continued to disciple him. I knew time was running out for Daniel. In spite of his newfound Christianity, and apparent change of behavior, his time to go before the judge approached. We prayed for him for favor, but as I have said, I fully expected him to end up behind bars. I felt that once that happened, he would probably turn his back on God, because God did not rescue him from the sentence he deserved. Besides, Daniel admitted that he had done everything he was accused of. He was finished… but God! Nothing is ever finished unless Christ declares it is finished!

I have no explanation for what happened in the courtroom. It defies logic and goes against the way things work in the justice system. On the day of his trial, Daniel stood before the judge, and apologized to the court and to those he had swindled. He said something like this.

> *Your honor, I am guilty of all that I am charged with and I am willing to accept my punishment. I am sorry for what I have done and ask for forgiveness. I have turned my life over to Christ, but I do not want to use that as an excuse to plead for leniency. I am in your hands, but I want you to know that even in prison, I will serve the Lord with all my heart for the rest of my life.*

The judge, in defiance of all logic, against all predictions and expectations (especially mine), told Daniel he knew he was guilty, but he had decided to dismiss all the charges - all thirty-two counts! To this day, nobody knows why the judge did that, except the judge himself. It could only have been the favor and grace of God speaking to the judge's heart. That day, Daniel walked out of court a free man. I have seen some people get what they needed from God and then turn their backs on him. Daniel did just the opposite. His deliverance fired up his faith and stoked his zeal. He was literally on fire for God! (As far as I know, he remains so to this day.)

The story does not end here. It gets even more amazing! Daniel was about to do what could only be done under the power and Lordship of Christ. Once again, it would challenge my belief... that his story was no more than just a pipe dream that was too ridiculous to happen. I have heard it said that God is an *"also God."* He can work a miracle now in one area, and He can also do it again in another. Daniel was about to give evidence to that. His life would prove the Scriptures to be true, regardless of natural circumstances. All things were about to become new, even Daniel's reputation!

> *(2 Corinthians 5:17 NKJV) "Therefore, if anyone is in Christ, he is a new creation; old things have passed away; behold, all things have become new."*

Daniel showed up at the door to my home one morning and I invited him into my office. (It is amazing how much I learned about people in that little room in my home in Fiji.) He said he was going into business to become a financial advisor. He would be structuring business deals between people for a fee. He wanted to do this within the same business community that he had worked all his fraudulent activities. I was a bit taken back. Such a thing was not even rational. Daniel said he was asking for my help for three reasons. First, I was his pastor. Second, he did not have a computer and I did. Third, he knew I had previous experience as a businessman and he respected my wisdom and wanted my help. My initial thought was, *"This guy is nuts! How does he expect anyone to trust him and commit their funds to his care?"* My second thought was, *"Well, I'm his pastor and my job is to encourage him, so I will go along with him, even though this is preposterous and I know it is a waste of time!"*

We subsequently met a couple times a week for months. Each time we met, we would craft a section of his business plan. Then, when he next came to the house, he would bring a yellow legal pad with new ideas and notes handwritten on it. We would discuss what he had written and I would transform it to the computer, editing the language as I went. It was becoming a very complex business plan. Eventually we had a solid, professional looking package he could use to make presentations. He took it and began trying to get people to engage in business investments with his guidance. Through it all, I believed he was wasting his time, asking people to trust him with their capital. I still thought he was naïve at best. Someone might listen to him out of politeness, but with his reputation, who would ever buy what he was selling?

Then one day he showed up at my door with a big smile on his face. Once again we sat in my office. He told me he had proposed to one of the wealthiest and most successful businessmen on the island that he help him prepare a plan to fund a business to supply vegetables to the resorts on the island and for export to other nations around the world. The man agreed, knowing full well who Daniel was! I had a hard time believing it, but there it was. It had to be the same favor and grace God placed on the judge. God proved He was an *"also God!"* I was amazed. I grudgingly accepted my chastisement from the Holy Spirit. I repented for my lack of faith. Now we began together to write the agreement for this new venture. I would then help him with the necessary paperwork that would follow. My attitude was still not right. I remember thinking, *"God, I don't have time for this. I am trying to pastor a church and run a ministry training school."* All I heard in my spirit was, *"Yes you have time. Just do it."* And so, we did!

To make a very long story a little bit shorter, this became the first of many business ventures Daniel successfully put together. In time, he became a pillar in the community, as well as the church. His successful stewardship of his business dealings became well known. He reestablished himself as completely trustworthy to do business with. As the months turned into years, he has been able to provide very well for his family and continues to bless the church.

The account of Daniel's successes is one of my best miracle testimonies from the mission field. It bears witness that all things truly are possible to those who believe. This was proven true in Daniel's display of newfound responsibility, combined with his trust in the Lord and willingness to do things the way God required. God performed His Word over Daniel. I saw it happen! I saw Daniel make landmark after landmark. How miraculous and unlimited the Lordship of Christ is! He will perform His Word over those who humbly submit to it. God's gift to me of Daniel was more than just participating in what he accomplished. Seeing God work through Daniel's willingness caused my faith to grow. It changed my expectations and altered my attitudes about others I have pastored or mentored who, in faith, stepped beyond their limitations. In spite of how they were when they came to me, I could trust that God would change them during the mentoring process. This was a lasting and liberating lesson. It took my faith to a new level. I would never be the same. We know God makes all things possible to him who believes. It is sometimes not so easy to believe. Nevertheless, it is true. God is always ready to do what He says He can do. Take it to the bank! Jesus is Lord.

Mentoring: Introducing new, often tough choices, which result in rethinking ones that have been previously made

(Mark 9:23 NKJV) "Jesus said to him, "If you can believe, all things are possible to him who believes.""

(Jeremiah 1:12 NKJV) "Then the LORD said to me, "You have seen well, for I am ready to perform My word.""

Make Him Lord and watch Him perform His Word!

Fifth Landmark: Compelling, Unwavering Service to God

Over the years, so many of my disciples have shown that special hunger to serve God. The desire to do something for the Lord with their lives was not an option. They were compelled. Anything else was unacceptable. In those times when they were not actively ministering, they experienced a frustration that could not be pacified or soothed. Eventually, we all find ourselves in those in-between times. Like me, you probably have had to live with this frustration from time to time (maybe even now). You need no explanation to understand what I am saying.

In addition to the in-between times, there are the difficult times. These are the inevitable experiences which demand clear and present sacrifice. Have you had them yet? If not, be sure you will. I have always felt that this compelling and unwavering desire to serve God is a gift He gave me when He called me. It has been a source of strength to me in difficult times. I have arrived at the point that serving Him is not an option. It is a commitment. It is my decision. It is even my need. This is the stuff our fifth landmark is made of. As I said in the beginning of this chapter, a landmark may be defined as a clearly recognizable sign of a significant historical event, or an achievement worth noting, taking place at a particular point in time. Let's add to this that life's landmarks provide us with evidence for our faith to stand strong. They cause us to remember the presence and power of God, as it had previously worked in us or our disciples. Such recollections give us the extra resolve and clear confidence to continue in what God is calling each of us to do. They energize the fires in our hearts and motivate us to press ahead to victory.

Life's landmarks provide us with evidence that our faith is standing strong.

Often, when I have encountered some significant roadblock to my own ministry, or when I am about to do something for God that I consider particularly difficult, I think of the passing of the prophet's mantle to Elisha. In the Second Chapter of the Book of Kings, we read of that final moment when Elijah is taken up to be with the Lord.

> *(2 Kings 2:11-15 NKJV) "Then it happened, as they continued on and talked, that suddenly a chariot of fire appeared with horses of fire, and separated the two of them; and Elijah went up by a whirlwind into heaven. {12} And Elisha saw it, and he cried out, "My father, my father, the chariot of Israel and its horsemen!" So he saw him no more. And he took hold of his own clothes and tore them into two pieces. {13} He also took up the mantle of Elijah that had fallen from him, and went back and stood by the bank of the Jordan. {14} Then he took the*

mantle of Elijah that had fallen from him, and struck the water, and said, "Where is the LORD God of Elijah?" And when he also had struck the water, it was divided this way and that; and Elisha crossed over. {15} Now when the sons of the prophets who were from Jericho saw him, they said, "The spirit of Elijah rests on Elisha." And they came to meet him, and bowed to the ground before him."

As Elisha watches, the Lord takes Elijah up into heaven. Elijah's mantle or cape is left behind and Elisha picks it up. He wraps himself in his mentor's cape and begins to walk into his destiny. He knows he will face formidable challenges to his abilities and authority, but his time with Elijah has prepared him. He is committed. There is no turning back. Look closely at what Elisha does when he encounters the first barrier he cannot cross. It is a river, and it blocks his way. This moment is about to become a landmark. Elisha will always be able to look back to it for assurance and inspiration. And so he takes Elijah's mantle from his shoulders and strikes the water with it. The power is not in the mantle, or in Elisha's actions. Nor is it in the one who used to wear it. Notice that Elisha does not say, *Where is the power of Elijah, or Where is the power of this mantle?* He has learned well from watching God work through his teacher. He says, *"Where is the Lord God of Elijah?"* This becomes a significant point of understanding. We are never far from the presence and power of the One who called us. We can call upon Him and He will hear. When He hears, He will answer. Teach your disciples this truth. You will have accomplished your assignment and equipped them to do the same!

(Mark 11:24 NKJV) "Therefore I say to you, whatever things you ask when you pray, believe that you receive them, and you will have them."

I am always encouraged by hearing of the landmarks in my disciples' lives. I am equally encouraged to know that their time with me was a life-changing landmark for them. I have learned that God provides us with landmarks in order to strengthen our ministries and give courage to those we mentor. Wouldn't you love to hear a report that your disciples encouraged themselves by thinking back to what they witnessed of your service to the Lord?

Let's review these five landmarks as we close the chapter.

1. Continuing Fruitfulness after they have left you
2. Reports of their Steadfast Character and Christ-likeness
3. Genuine Humility in the Conduct of their Lives
4. Indisputable Signs of the Lordship of Christ
5. Compelling, Unwavering Service to God

What is Mentoring?

(From the definitions given in the pages of this chapter, above)

Mentoring is your best service to others to insure they will embrace and fulfill their destinies. Mentoring challenges all involved with new ideas and examples. As a result, everyone finds themselves rethinking ideas they previously believed to be valid. This leads to what are often tough choices and sometimes even tougher changes.

Chapter 6

How will you Answer the Rain?

A significant part of your mentoring process will be to help your disciples understand how to respond to those inevitable times of stress, disappointment, and even apparent failure. You and I have experienced these things. They will too. Equipping them for these times is part of your assignment as their mentor. Simply teaching them what the Bible says does not guarantee their future responses to these pressures will be correct and effective. There must be something more they can catch in their time with you. I have learned, first hand, that difficult times will come when we least expect them. They will never be convenient. They can, however, be utilized as a valuable learning experience. My pastor, Dr. Tom Peters, has often said,

"God can take a devastating crisis and turn it into a blessing."

Our challenge as mentors is to walk through our own disappointments in ways that demonstrate faith and perseverance to others. If we are trusting and faithful in those times when trouble rains down upon us, and if we refuse to give in to the circumstances, those watching will be apprehended by what they see. They will gain the inspiration, and the tools to go successfully beyond their own inevitable moments of stress, disappointment and apparent failure. If you will recall in Chapter 4, I testified to my own struggles in the grip of a life-threatening illness. I would like to remind you of a powerful truth I gave you about this experience. The doctor's report and my reaction to it became my unlikely opportunity to snatch victory from the jaws of defeat. As I said in Chapter 4, my appointment with cancer was not my last appointment. It became an opportunity for another appointment - an appointment with God. It began what would be the most intensely personal encounter with God I have ever experienced. The depths of that life-changing encounter were even more significant than the miracle of my victory over the disease. When the Lord showed up, I was gripped by His grace. It was overwhelming. His loving presence was singularly personal toward me. In His hands, I persevered to my victory.

The lesson went beyond the victory. It was a lesson in the overwhelming value of the intense, caring presence of God. I will always remember that He never let go of me, even in the worst of it. Your difficulty may not be as serious, but it is nevertheless, very real to you. When you are in the grip of your trouble, let yourself be gripped by His grace. God has the stronger hand. He will always prevail.

When you are in the grip of your trouble, let yourself be gripped by His grace. God has the stronger hand. He will always prevail.

Here is another lesson. If you live in His grip before the trouble, you can stay safely in His grip during the trouble. When you are beyond the trouble, His fingerprints will be on your victory... and on you! One of the opportunities of mentoring is to model a lifestyle of closeness to God. If you walk with Him and trust Him with all your heart, then your attitudes, your words and your actions will catch the hearts of those watching. They will become more like their teacher. Everyone will become more like Christ!

(Isaiah 40:10-11 NKJV) "Behold, the Lord GOD shall come with a strong hand, And His arm shall rule for Him; Behold, His reward is with Him, And His work before Him. {11} He will feed His flock like a shepherd; He will gather the lambs with His arm, And carry them in His bosom, And gently lead those who are with young."

(Isaiah 59:1 NKJV) "Behold, the Lord's hand is not shortened, That it cannot save; Nor His ear heavy, That it cannot hear."

꧁ Fifty Students in a Rainstorm ꧂

As part of our curriculum in the School of Urban Missions in Fiji, we had extracurricular requirements for almost every day. In the afternoons, the students were all busy with planting cell groups, doing hospital visitation, and evangelizing. We had about twenty Bible studies going on in various offices and businesses around the city. There was also a great amount of street evangelism happening in the most unlikely of places. We had an aggressive ministry to the homeless and the prostitutes who hung around on the street next to our church. We were a busy bunch!

Ever so often, we planned an evangelistic outreach in the park, which was central to downtown Suva. It was just off the harbor and was surrounded by many of the city's busiest offices and shops. At the very edge of the park, was a band shell where we planned to hold our outreach. It was only about a hundred feet from the only McDonald's in Suva and was a popular gathering place. Needless to say, we anticipated a large crowd would be there when we kicked off our program. For weeks, the students had spent hours and hours preparing for the crusade. They had rehearsed their skits, practiced their music, coordinated the testimonies, prepared short sermons, assigned follow-up ministers to be among the people, and done all those things necessary to make for a successful program. The students knew it was going to be a great time - a great demonstration of the power of the Gospel. They could hardly wait! They were excited, highly motivated and ready. They knew they were a relentless, unstoppable force for the Gospel… that is until they encountered the one variable that could stop them in their tracks. I am talking about the weather.

If I had to describe Suva to you with only one word, it would have to be "wet." Suva is a city where it rains most days. When it rains, the windows of heaven truly open up. I can recall my wife hanging our clothes out to dry on our back porch and after a few days, having to bring them back in, as wet as when they went out, to be washed again. Everywhere you looked in Suva, there was an ever-present green and black patina of mold and mildew. Walking through mud was a common experience. Rain and heavy humidity was just a part of life.

On the morning of the outreach, our students arrived, set up on the stage and made their sound system ready. As the music began, they suddenly found themselves facing a torrential downpour. The park quickly emptied, except for a handful of die-hard souls who had taken refuge under the trees which dotted the landscape. Among these hardy souls were Nancy and me. We stood under an umbrella watching the pouring rain flood the grounds. It was washing away all of our students' expectations for a glorious day. They bravely tried to continue their program, but it was next to impossible. What could be done?

Throughout the year I had taught them that with God all things are possible. We had become a bunch of fiery, faith-filled fanatics for Jesus. We believed in the power of prayer and the authority of the believer. As their leader and mentor, I knew it was time to put feet to my faith. Holy anger was rising up inside of me. There was no way that this rain would be allowed to stop our work for the kingdom. After all, it was for the glory of God. I would stand on my faith and declare a thing or two!

I confidently moved out into the downpour and strode up to the band shell. I walked up the steps onto the stage. I interrupted the student who was doing his best to sing through the misery the downpour was inflicting on him. I confidently took the microphone out of his hands. It was time for an open show of the power of God in the face of the enemy. With all the boldness I could muster, fully believing that God would honor my fiery passion, I shouted into the microphone, *"In the mighty name of Jesus of Nazareth, I command this rain to stop - right now!"* Everyone was watching. Everyone heard the faith-filled command, spoken in the rightfully delegated authority of our Commander-in-Chief, the Lord Jesus Christ. Everyone fully expected the rain to stop. I was chief among them. We just knew the sun was about to shine. As I have written previously, expect the unexpected. I gave the microphone back to the student and confidently strode back to my place under the tree. We waited for the rain to stop. It would be any moment now. It rained harder. We waited some more. It rained even harder. It never slowed down. It rained all day. Finally, we packed up our gear and went back to the church, soaked to the bone.

It was the following week and I was teaching class one morning. The students were feeling down and discouraged because of the disappointment we all experienced the previous week. Now there was a deluge of doubt circulating in the class. In the middle of the lesson (I cannot remember what I was teaching), one of my students raised his hand.

> *"Pastor, why did the rain continue last week? You took authority over it and commanded it to stop. We know the power of God is in us to do such things. Why didn't it stop?"*

That got everyone's attention. I could see the whole class was now pondering the same question.

It was a good question. I thought about it. Why wasn't my prayer answered? Why didn't it stop raining? Why wasn't my authority effective from the stage that day? After all, we were after souls for Jesus. We were about the work of the kingdom. Shouldn't the rain have stopped? What could I say to them? It was one of those times when God intervenes and speaks wonderful things, for in that moment the Holy Spirit burned something into me. I heard the Spirit of God say, *"That is the wrong question."* It was revelation. It was liberating and exciting. It was wrong because it was the kind of question that could never be answered. Who were we to question God or put such demands on Him? The farmers in the fields just outside of town might have been praying for the very rain we were praying against! The right question should have been, *How will we respond to what happened in that rainstorm? With what will our faith answer the rainstorm?* I could not contain myself. I had to let it out! Listen to my reply. Let the spirit of what I told my students ignite something in your heart, just as it did theirs. Then, take it to the people you will mentor. Here is what I said.

> *"If we spend the next two weeks preparing for another evangelistic crusade... and set our equipment up on that stage in the park... and begin our program and the heavy rain comes again... I will march up to the platform, take the microphone*

and command the rain to stop, in the name of Jesus. I will expect it to stop!

If the rain does not stop, but becomes another torrential downpour, I will go home soaked, but I will go, knowing that God is faithful and I did the right thing.

And if we spend another two weeks preparing for another evangelistic crusade...and set our equipment up on that same stage in that same park... and begin our program and the rain comes again... I will still march up to the platform. I will again take the microphone and command the rain to stop, in the name of Jesus! And I will expect it to stop. That is what faith is all about!"

When my students heard my reply to the question, there was a moment of silence. Then, there came a spontaneous roar - an eruption of great joy. They jumped from their chairs and began celebrating. Spontaneous praise broke out. They began to shout and run and declare the goodness of God. It was truly a sight to behold! What happened? They simply understood what I was saying, which was this. It is never about God's performance or lack of performance. Nor is it about whether the prayer is answered. It is not about results or consequences. It is simply about believing God is who He says He is and can always do what He says He can do. It is about living a life of faith, regardless of the outcome. Our responsibility is to do what faith demands, to trust God in spite of the circumstances. It is about uncompromising, stubborn, single-minded faith. Job said it best, when in the midst of incredibly difficulties, he told his friends, *"Though He slay me, yet will I trust Him." (Job 13:15a NKJV)*

My Fijian students now understood that regardless of how many times we would endure the rains, I would repeatedly persist in commanding them to stop. Whether or not the rains stopped, I would not stop. We are to believe God, without Him having to prove anything. The students were moved to new places in their faith. I will never forget hearing their shouts and watching them dance. It was the kind of faith-filled pandemonium that will terrify the devil and convince him to go somewhere easier! I learned that day that the most important thing I could be to them was a person of fiery, ferocious, unfailing faith. They realized faith is not about results. It is about unwavering trust in God. Dr. Charles Stanley and Dr. Joseph Stowell both have defined faith this way:

> "Faith simply believes, then behaves accordingly and lets God manage the outcome."[16]

Faith is not about results. It is about unwavering trust in God.

Take this message to the people God gives you to mentor. Tell them faith never gives in, never gives up and never gives out! Tell them that sometimes you have to shout before the walls come down and keep shouting until they do! Your students will catch your faith, just as my students caught mine. They will be history makers and devil breakers!

(Hebrews 11:6a NKJV) "But without faith it is impossible to please Him..."

---

[16] Dr. Charles Stanley's In Touch TV ministry - Also found in the excellent book by Dr. Joseph Stowell, entitled Shepherding the Church. (Moody Press, 1997.)

(Mark 9:23 NKJV) "Jesus said to him, "If you can believe, all things are possible to him who believes.""

Mentoring: The sum of three parts: (1) teaching what they need to know, (2) helping them practice what they have been taught, and (3) imparting to them the faith to grow and walk in victory - Always give preference to the third part, impartation of faith. Without faith, it is impossible to please God, but with it, all things are possible!

ꟿ Roti from Heaven ꟿ

As the school year continued, for most of our students, the issue of school fees loomed like a dark cloud before the storm. They typically had come from impoverished backgrounds and rural locations. They had been serving in the Christian Mission Fellowship (CMF), living mostly by faith. A great percentage of our students were staying in Suva with relatives or friends who provided for their basic needs. It was a common occurrence for a student to go to the bus stop and wait, praying until someone came along offering to pay the bus fare to school. Payment of their school fees was required by the CMF as a condition of the students' graduation. To understand this, you have to know that it took great faith to start the CMF. It took that same great faith for its many church planters and evangelists to sustain themselves in the typically hard and unfriendly places they went. Faith was the primary issue in their lives. It was life-sustaining for them. I discovered that my own faith would constantly be stretched and could not be compromised. The students looked to me to inspire them! Yes, God has a sense of humor because it was quite the opposite. They had far more faith than I did and I learned a great deal about it from them.

We had one couple who really struggled financially to survive their year at school. They did not have the local connections other students had. Just putting food on their table was a test for them. They were among those who had to pray for their bus fare on a regular basis. One day they came to me and explained their problem with the lack of money (which I was already aware of). They did not know how they would pay their school fees, but they had an idea and wanted my permission. It had to do with our daily break in the mornings, when we stopped classes and everyone had tea from a big pot. Sometimes someone would bring fresh bread or hot rolls from the bakery on the first floor, just below the church. It might be a student who happened to have a few extra dollars, or perhaps a member of the church who wanted to bless the students. What made this time so significant was that we also invited the homeless and a number of street prostitutes who hung out around our building. We used this time of fellowship to minister to them, even as we took our break. It was a very fruitful mission.

The couple asked me if they could make roti, a popular Indian wrap-like sandwich, and sell them during our daily tea break. They believed that the proceeds would help them pay their school fees. It was the only way they could see to do this. I admired their resourcefulness. It would be a hardship on them just to prepare the roti every day. After all, they were already extremely busy and had little time available. At first glance, the plan seemed to be workable - a great solution. However, it presented me with a dilemma. During the day, the church doubled as the school's offices, library and classroom. I had established a rule for our church that nothing would be sold within its walls. I have personally felt the house of God to be sacred and took Jesus' overturning of the money changers' tables to be a model I would always follow. The Gospel is free and anything we provided within the walls of our church would be a reflection of this.

I knew they had the need. I even felt the Holy Spirit had moved them in the direction of making the roti. What could I do? I thought about it and knew I had to say no to selling roti in the church. You should have seen their faces when I told them. They were struck down with disappointment. As I said, disappointment is always an opportunity for another appointment, an appointment with God. This would be the beginning of a great faith experience that blessed them, encouraged me and was a testimony to the whole class. I said to them, *"Listen, God wants to provide for you. Here is what I would like you to consider. Make your roti every day. Bring them to school and, in faith, set them out on a tray. Put an empty bowl next to the roti. Say nothing about any price for them. Do not make any signs for the bowl. Just pray and ask God to touch people's hearts and believe that He will fill the bowl with money. Would you agree to try this?"* They thought about it for a moment and agreed. They would trust their faith.

The roti quickly disappeared from the tray every day. They were a tasty blessing and made our tea breaks special. Nobody said anything about the bowl, sitting there next to the roti, but everyone knew it was there. As the days and weeks went by, the bowl always seemed to have money in it at the end of the tea break. I can report to you that they were able to pay their school fees and graduated with a great understanding of how faith will fill your bowl! It was a lesson we all came to appreciate. Here is what the roti taught us. I like to put it in three parts.

1. The Lesson

When there seem to be barriers you cannot cross, turn to God, give away something of yourself as an act of faith, just to bless somebody. Ask God for His provision. Believe He will be who He says He is. His name is Jehovah Jireh (God our Provider). Then, watch Him perform His Word over you! Faith will fill your bowl!

2. The Side Effects

Someone will be blessed entirely apart from your need. Some of the students had no money to buy roti. Nevertheless, they could enjoy them every day. Others were able to put something in the bowl from time to time. God had ways of providing for them, so they could fill the bowl. Then there were the unfortunates, the prostitutes and the homeless, who were invited to have tea with us every day. They simply experienced acceptance and felt the love of God. They were fed, accepted and valued without the usual judgment they endured on the streets. They were important and valuable to us. I will never know how all this influenced and encouraged them to escape from the misery they lived in, but I know some received the Lord into their hearts and made themselves available for God to work in their lives.

3. The End Result

As the students took part in our daily love feast of roti, they learned firsthand, that faith in action is a winner! When they added this to the lesson of the prayer that did not stop the pouring rain, their understanding of faith and all its power significantly deepened. The roti were tasty morsels from heaven! They took everyone to new places in Christ. We all became even more dangerous to the devil!

I have given you two examples of faith in action. In the first, the students saw me refuse to diminish my faith, in spite of my unanswered prayers. They saw the power in believing God that goes beyond the answer and stands in the midst of its expectations. They learned that our perspective ought to reflect our understanding of Who He is and who we are in Him, regardless of how things might turn out. In the second example, the students observed two of their own, making a decision to act in faith, believing God's Word and seeing their prayers answered. These two trusting people made some roti and freely gave them as an every-day act of charity and blessing toward others. God miraculously turned that combination of giving, grace and good roti into paid-up school fees.

Teach those you mentor that God is to be celebrated regardless of the outcome of their prayers. Tell them never to stop believing. He is forever faithful and always has our well-being in His heart. Teach them that if they will take the ordinary and apply faith to it, it will become the stuff of miracles. God will take what they have put their hands to and multiply it, just like Jesus did with the loaves and fishes.

> *(Luke 6:38 NKJV) "Give, and it will be given to you: good measure, pressed down, shaken together, and running over will be put into your bosom. For with the same measure that you use, it will be measured back to you."*

ꕤ "I've got it - Another Missionary!" ꕤ

I want to share with you a third example of faith in action from my time in Fiji. This one impressed me so much I have never forgotten it and I often think about it when I have decisions to make. It was a lesson in faith that came from the heart of one of the elders in our church there. Here is how it happened.

We had been doing really well with our church. It was rapidly growing. We had recently moved the church and Bible school into our new location on the second floor of the Harbour Centre in downtown Suva (which I spoke of in the story of the roti, above). We all were incredibly enthusiastic about what was happening in the church. The people were eager participants in the life of the church. Everything that Nancy and I believed our church ought to be seemed to be coming to pass. There was no lack. We had plenty of willing people to do the work of the ministry. Tithes and offerings were coming in well. It was a time of favor from God and blessings among the people. We were on a roll!

It was my usual pattern to meet with the church elders one evening each week at our home. Nancy would prepare tea and dessert and we would eat and have a great time together. Then we would fellowship until it was time to get down to business. The bonding between us as elders was incredibly strong and edifying. We would pray, and then I would teach them the principles and skills of leadership that I wanted to impart to them. Finally we would get down to the business of the church and make the decisions necessary for the issues at hand. When we were finished, they usually stayed well into the night and it took about three or four goodbyes to end the evening. Then they would usually walk home, continuing their fellowship well into the early morning.

Much of our success as a church came because of the way these men had taken personal responsibility for the church. I made a determination from the very beginning that I would share the leadership of the church and its decision making processes with my elders for everything except those spiritual issues I felt belonged to me as the senior pastor. They were surprised at my willingness to do so, as their previous cultural and church experiences were quite the opposite. Typically, Fijian society, including church life, was very much top-down with a strong leader at the top. There was not much power sharing. When I asked them to accept the responsibility to share the leadership with me, they embraced the opportunity and it was one of the best mentoring decisions I have made. They just did a great job! They were handling most of the daily church life without having to involve me. This left me without much distraction and gave me plenty of time to concentrate on my weekly preaching, leadership training and Bible school teaching. I remained a strong leader and did not abdicate my authority (and there were times when I had to exercise it), but I did delegate it with extremely fruitful results.

On one particular Thursday evening, we were discussing our desire to add some new ministry activities to the church. Doing so would cost us a significant amount above our present weekly budget. There was no extra money. For quite a while, we kicked around ideas on raising money. Finally, I suggested we go home and pray about it. We could take up the discussion at our next meeting. Everyone agreed and we tabled it. A week went by, and we again met at our house, went through our normal routine until it was time to discuss the issue we had tabled the previous week. I asked whether anyone had any ideas about how to raise the money to pay for the new ministry activities. None of them seemed to have an answer. So we decided to pray about it for a while. One of our elders was Bentley Wan Chong. He was a banker and had a lovely family. He was half Chinese and half Fijian. After a few minutes, Bentley shouted, *"I've got it! Let's find another missionary to support!"* There was dead silence. We all looked at each other as though he was a genius. At that moment, something when off in all our spirits together. It was revelation. *"That's it,"* I said. Everyone instantly agreed. Instead of trying to raise money, we would give money and add another missionary to the list of those we already supported. *"Where would the money come from to do that?"* someone asked. *"Let's believe God for it!"* someone else said. There were smiles all around. We agreed and said our three or four goodbyes to end the evening.

We determined to find another missionary we could support and immediately began to do so. We never made an issue out of it before the church. We never announced anything publicly, or tried to raise additional funds. It was an issue of agreement before nine men who would trust God. The very next week, without any apparent cause, giving in the church increased dramatically and stayed at a level which provided for both the new missionary and the new ministry activities. It was faith in action and God responded. He demonstrated that He can do exceedingly abundantly above all we can ask or think, and He can do it in more than one direction at a time. He is an "also" God! He answered our need, and also caused us to answer the need of one of His valued servants on the mission field. His ways are higher than ours. He will often require us to pray and submit our ways to His. You cannot out-give God, but it sure is fun to try! Teach your disciples this lesson.

Six Key Lessons or Faith Principles

I began this chapter by drawing your attention to the need to prepare your disciples for the stresses, disappointments and even apparent failures they will encounter in their service to the Lord. By now, from what you have read, it should be obvious that the answer to these times of difficulty has everything to do with faith. If our disciples are successful in finishing the race God puts before them, they will need to be equipped with strong faith. Nothing else will see them through. Let's look at some of the key lessons or principles we derived from the narratives, above.

1. Faith is not about outcomes. It does not prove itself by the results we see. Faith is about understanding who He is and who we are in Him, regardless of how things might turn out.
2. When we make the decision to act in faith, we are to expect God to respond and answer our prayers.
3. God will take our every-day acts of giving and give us back His miraculous blessings.
4. You cannot out-give God. He will always out-give you!
5. God can do so much more than we expect, and He can do it in more than one direction at a time. He is an "also" God!
6. Faith never gives in. Faith never gives up. Faith never gives out. These three truths form what is perhaps the most important of these six key lessons. They are the thread that runs through all the faith lessons and testimonies that have ever been written.

It is paramount that we give the exercise of faith the strongest priority in the mentoring process. Faith is not an acquired skill though I believe it needs to be practiced. It is not a result of high intellect or education, though I believe God can teach us a great deal about it. It is not an application of technology or technique, though there are some ways of exercising faith that are certainly more effective than others. Faith, as the Bible defines it, is simply a gift we are given by God to empower us to believe in Him and what He has said. It is a precious gift. We are asked and indeed, required to steward it, so it will grow and become increasingly effective.

(Luke 17:5-6 NKJV) "And the apostles said to the Lord, "Increase our faith." {6} So the Lord said, "If you have faith as a mustard seed, you can say to this mulberry tree, 'Be pulled up by the roots and be planted in the sea,' and it would obey you."

In Luke 17, Jesus compares a tiny mustard seed to the potential within even a little faith. The gift of faith, which begins in such a small way, can be stewarded to become so much more. It can grow from small beginnings to great endings! The Lord gives us the key to releasing this faith. He says, *"If you have faith as a mustard seed, you can say..."*

Faith lies dormant until it is released by our words. When we speak words of faith over a situation, God releases a supernatural response to what we have said. It is so important to guard our words in the presence of those we mentor. There are always spiritual principles and forces at work in what we say (positive or negative), and these are easily caught by those who hear us. This works both ways. We can mentor people into weak faith, doubt and even unbelief with just the pattern of our words. We can also mentor them into great faith and a belief that all things are possible to Him who believes.

(Mark 9:23 NKJV) "Jesus said to him, "If you can believe, all things are possible to him who believes.""

Mentoring: A display of the mentor's faith which God uses to increase the strength of the belief systems of those who are watching, listening and learning

I read a story once that stuck with me. I do not know its origin, but I have been holding onto it for years. On occasion, it has helped me to keep going when the going was getting rough and I could not see how things could end favorably. The story illustrates two Biblical truths. First, there is divine purpose in our faith challenges; and second, the most important ending to any faith challenge is not the change in our circumstances, but the change in us. Here is the story.

People are like Potatoes.

When potatoes are harvested they are spread out and sorted according to size – small, medium and large. After they have been sorted, they are bagged and loaded onto trucks. One farmer never bothered to sort his potatoes. Yet he was making more money from his potatoes than the others who took their potatoes to the market. One of his puzzled competitors finally asked him, *"What is your secret?"* He said, *"It's simple. I just load up my wagon with potatoes and take the roughest road into town. During the two-hour trip, the little potatoes always fall to the bottom. The medium potatoes land in the middle, and the big potatoes rise to the top."*

Life is like a wagon full of potatoes. The big potatoes rise to the top on rough roads, and tough, persevering, Christ-committed people rise to the top in rough times. Tough times never last, but tough people do.[17]

(James 1:2-4 NKJV) "My brethren, count it all joy when you fall into various trials, {3} knowing that the testing of your

[17] Source unknown to the author

faith produces patience. {4} But let patience have its perfect work, that you may be perfect and complete, lacking nothing."

I do not suggest you look at the people you are mentoring as though they were potatoes. Each of them is unique and uniquely made. They are feeling, thinking, complex human beings who are incredibly valuable. But the lesson of the story can well be applied to them and to each of us. The lesson is simple, yet profound; the trip may be rough and tumble, but when it is over we will end up on top.

Optimistic Faith: Heaven's Currency in a Mentor's Pocket

Leadership, and especially the mentoring part of it, ought to be a business of constant optimism. I must admit, nobody (and certainly not me) is always optimistic in the face of life's challenges. Nevertheless, we are responsible to model a hopeful confidence. We ought to try our best to do so. Along with the challenging times, there will be times when opportunities for the good things in life come our way. These demand the same optimistic faith. In either case, God is the same in the sunshine as He is in the rain! I have had many opportunities to remind myself of this. Invariably, the people I led observed my reactions. I learned that they were likely to imitate what they saw. Faith functions the same whether it is working through our troubles or taking us to our blessings.

Faith works in the sunshine just as well as in the rain!

℘☙ In the Heart of the City ℘☙

I would like to share another story to finish this chapter. It is about how faith took Nancy, me, and our church to an impossible blessing. In the process, it affected the faith of our church forever. It was an opportunity for us to witness God seriously challenging, and then answering our collective faith. It required a dose of highly optimistic faith. Defeat was not an option! Here is how it went.

As I previously mentioned, the beginnings of our church took place in a hotel bar. We quickly discovered that the church offerings were small, averaging about two hundred Fijian dollars a week. The first one hundred dollars of it went to pay the hotel for the use of the bar on Sunday morning. Out of the remaining one hundred dollars, we fed and housed our then six full-time young men who were in training for ministry, and paid all our other expenses. It was a stretch!

A few months went by and we had grown to about sixty people. We filled the place up and there were no more seats available. The people began to grasp my message of faith, integrity and good success. They were taking ownership of the church and becoming truly excited about what God was doing. The word was getting out around town. It was a wonderful time. We had things going well. It was happening, literally at the gates of hell and it was obvious that these particular gates would not prevail against God's church. However, I knew we needed to find another place to call home. It would have to be a facility where we could realize our dreams for the kind of church we hungered to see God build. Now it was time for Nancy and me to take that step of faith and do what was beyond us to do, to find that facility. We had been very specific in our prayers. We asked God for a suitable facility "in the heart of the city." Nancy and I began walking around in the center of downtown Suva, looking for the right building. We were focused. We knew there was something out there for us, but it was frustrating trying to find something we could afford that had the right location.

One day, we were walking in front of the city's largest department store (not to be confused with what you would expect in a Western setting). It was in an extremely busy and well populated part of downtown. It was near all the shops, just a few blocks from the market and in easy walking distance of the bus terminal. As we walked past the door to the department store, we had one of those moments that was so supernatural we could hardly believe it. Directly across the street was a two story building which was called the Harbour Centre. The first floor was filled with small shops. On the second floor was a large, vacant space. Painted on the side of the building, over the windows on the second floor, was a sign that read, "In the Heart of the City." Yes, it read word for word what we had been praying for - "In the Heart of the City!" God had labeled the building before we ever prayed, and then put the label in our hearts. It was a breathtaking moment for us.

We discovered the building was owned and operated by the government. We found out who to see and visited the government's property manager, who was quite polite and receptive to our inquiry. He told us that he was about to advertise the vacant space for the following week in the hopes of renting it to a number of small tenants. He said that if he did not get any responses through the weekend, he would be willing to rent us the entire space. We began to pray. Sure enough, the week went by and nobody tried to contact him. It was surely the favor with God. We met with him again and because there had been no response, he expressed his willingness to rent it to us. That was the successful conclusion of step one for our faith. Step two would be more challenging. He was asking for eighteen hundred Fiji dollars per month, plus taxes, which totaled two thousand a month. We would be required to come up with a ten-fold increase in the amount we paid for rent - every month! We shared all this with our elders. These wonderful men know how to touch God in prayer! There would be no doubting or wavering. Defeat was not an option! We believed we had been divinely directed to that sign on the wall. If God provided it, He would pay for it. We all prayed and everyone had peace.

We let the people know what the Lord had provided. As usual, we were careful not to pressure anyone. I have always had very strong principles about not pressuring people into giving. I would trust that they would hear from God, and each week would tithe and give according to what God put in their hearts. It would be more than enough. The elders, Nancy and I had front row seats to the miracle. Week after week the money came in. We never were a day late with our rent. Had we not returned to America upon completion of our commitment, and turned the church over to the next pastor, we were hoping to buy the building. The lesson to be learned from all this is that faith speaks to the rain without wavering, but it also speaks just as confidently in the sunshine… and defeat is not an option!

When optimistic faith springs into action, defeat is not an option!

Faith is the currency of the Kingdom of God. However, the difference between faith and the world's currency is basic and profound. You can easily spend the world's currency. It matters not whether it is a euro, a ruble, or a dollar. The world's currency disappears as we spend it. In God's economy, however, there is no way to spend or be indebted by the currency of faith. You can only invest it and get a return. Its value is guaranteed and backed by the King and all His treasure!

- You can bank on it.
- You can multiply it.
- You can withdraw it, if you have deposited it and stored it up.
- You can cash it in for what you hoped for, and yet you will not have spent it.
- It is backed by the infallible, fully trustworthy promise of our forever faithful Father.
- It is not subject to deflation, inflation or instability. It does not have a variable exchange rate. It always is worth what God says it is worth. It remains fully valued into eternity.

Faith is a very different medium of exchange than what the world offers. Teach those you mentor to know the value of heaven's currency. Then teach them how to invest it wisely, to share it with others and cause it to multiply.

What is Mentoring?

(From the definitions given in the pages of this chapter, above)

Mentoring is the sum of three parts - (1) teaching what they need to know, (2) helping them practice what they have been taught, and (3) imparting to them the faith to grow and walk in victory. Always give preference to the third part - impartation of faith.

Mentoring is always to be a display of the mentor's faith, which God uses to increase the strength of the belief systems of those who are watching, listening and learning.

Chapter 7

Inconvenient Love

The Unlovely

(1 John 2:9-11 NKJV) "He who says he is in the light, and hates his brother, is in darkness until now. {10} He who loves his brother abides in the light, and there is no cause for stumbling in him. {11} But he who hates his brother is in darkness and walks in darkness, and does not know where he is going, because the darkness has blinded his eyes."

There will be times when you find yourself mentoring people you have neither chosen nor desired. They will be those who God chooses for you, not the ones you choose for yourself. He will bring them across your path and ask you to commit yourself to them. You may feel no affinity for them. Your feelings may be quite the opposite. You may even feel distaste and the desire to distance yourself from them. However, these are points in time when there is kingdom business to be done. In these times, you will have to look deeply within yourself. God will ask you to surrender your feelings, to crucify them and embrace your opportunity to be compassionate, merciful and yes, even loving. You will have to see through the eyes of Christ, and not your own eyes. Regardless of what your mind, will and emotions want to tell you, you will be confronted with the challenge - will you freely embrace them as Christ would? Will you go beyond what your feelings want or do not want? Will you love those who seem to you to be so unlovely?

ꕥ Chandan ꕥ

When I began my relationship with Chandan, I was overwhelmed with distaste and a sense of inconvenience. I had within myself, a clear and uncomfortable tension between what my emotions were saying and what my spirit was hearing. I kept my heart open, but my mind and emotions grasped for the selfishness and pride that infects every one of us. Ultimately, I would learn to first suppress and then reject the discomfort, inconvenience and just plain irritation my flesh was happy to keep before me. It was a struggle to embrace compassion and find God's mercy within me. I knew what was right. I knew what God required, and so I determined to let my actions dictate my feelings, until it would no longer be a struggle. I surrendered to mercy and grace. I let it have its way with me. It was the right decision. I overcame and grew to see Chandan through the eyes of the Lord. He became somebody special to me.

Loving the unlovely requires complete surrender to grace.

Because of what this internal battle did in and for me, I will forever be grateful for Chandan. No, he was not to become a spiritual son whom I would mentor into a great minister. He was a poor soul, lost in his misfortune, but found in the amazing grace of the Almighty. He was precious to God and I knew he would have to become precious to me. Otherwise, I would have been the greatest of hypocrites. What happened to bring us together was simply that he recognized I was his gift from God, and in time, and equally as simply, I recognized he was my gift from God.

Mentoring: The exchange of living gifts from God - gifts of each other, to one another

Our First Encounter

It was at the conclusion of one of our Sunday worship services, and I was praying for people at the altar. One of the women in our church brought this sad looking man up for prayer. He had an air of hopelessness about him and I quickly learned he was indeed living on the streets. He was poorly dressed and obviously in both physical and mental distress. We often had homeless people in attendance in our churches. Sadly, homelessness is universal around the world. I prayed for him without too much thought about who he was or what he was going through. I cannot tell you what I prayed, but I remember how touched he was by the moment. Looking back, I only wish I was as touched as he was. As I prayed, he fell to his knees against me and began weeping. When I was done praying for him, I extracted myself from his grip and moved on to finish the service.

This brief encounter was the first of several years of meetings with Chandan. He never missed a Sunday. In time, I became well acquainted with his situation, his problems and the tragedies of his life. He was shipwrecked and surely about to drown in his circumstances. Without my knowing it at the time, God had thrown him a life preserver. Little did I know that I was hanging onto the end of its rope and God was making it my task to reel him in. He was in God's grip and was about to be placed in mine too.

As time went by, and as I was privileged to get to know Chandan quite well, I began to understand him and gradually learned his life's story. I was amazed to find out that his past included an education from some of the world's best institutions of higher learning. In spite of this, here he was, now homeless and seemingly without hope of any improvement in his circumstances. He was barely surviving on the streets of New York City. His life was surely a dead end. I cannot tell you exactly when my attitude toward him changed, but my heart gradually began to soften toward him, until I saw him in a very different way than when I first met him. God was working on me big time! I often found myself taking hour-long subway trips, good weather or bad, to meet with him. We always met at the main branch of the New York Public Library. Chandan spent his mornings there, always in the same chair at the same table. I was amazed to realize he was doing some sophisticated research in international politics.

When I would meet Chandan, he would smile, give me a hug and put all his papers in the bag he always carried. Then we would go to lunch (usually in a small sandwich shop). Typically, we spent about an hour together talking about the issues of his life. Our time together was always an emotional time for him. He could hardly believe I went to the trouble of traveling to town just to be with him. Sometimes, as we were sitting and eating, all I could do was listen to him, trying to find something encouraging to say. Many times I could not think of anything helpful to say. However, it was at these times that God spoke to me about the things my wife and I, and the church could do to improve his situation. We did all we could. Before long it became apparent to me that in our meetings at the sandwich shop, there were three of us at the table - Chandan, me and Jesus. These were divine appointments, and would have divinely authored and divinely enabled results. Our lunches were at the banqueting table of God's love for him and yes, even for me. When I think back to those times, I cannot help but be drawn to the reality of the Scripture from The Song of Solomon.

(Song of Songs 2:4 NKJV) "He brought me to the banqueting house, And his banner over me was love."

What never fails to humble and impress me is how God used those lunches to display His banner of immeasurable love over both Chandan and me. God has just such a banner for each of us. It covers us and declares His intentions toward us. The message of this divinely placed banner is always the same - love, grace, mercy, compassion and faithfulness. We are all His children. We are all loved. How could I look at Chandan in any other way than as my brother, equally loved, equally as valuable to God as I am?

One-on-one mentoring encounters are divine appointments - never for two, always for three!

Every Sunday, Chandan soaked his soul in my sermons. I watched him week after week, as he gained new strength and found renewed faith. He took the Word of God into his heart. He made room for it and embraced it each time he heard it. It would affect him forever. Whenever I spoke with him, I made in my practice to speak of God's faithfulness and of how the Lord was willing and able to change his every circumstance, yes, even his. Chandan began to see there was hope. I spent so many hours, both with him, and also alone, trying to discern what God had planned for him. I knew that if he would cooperate with what I asked of him, and be willing to trust the Lord, things would surely change for the better. Well, things did change for Chandan. As they did, I watched him draw closer and closer to God. Our church was able to help him get good medical and dental care. The treatment he received for his health problems eventually bore fruit. His health vastly improved. Many of the problems that plagued him gradually began to fade. He began to speak of his life in hopeful terms. It was not easy for him. However, in many ways, he was becoming an overcomer.

The church assisted Chandan in moving into an apartment. He found work where his employers, who graciously looked past his circumstances, appreciated him for his faithfulness. We did whatever we could. It was never convenient, but always a blessing. I can remember taking a two-hour trip to pay his dental bill. I remember how cold it was on so many winter mornings waiting for him on the steps of the library so we could sit together for a bite to eat, or go together to get his medication from the pharmacy. These and many other small victories were just the physical things we were able to do for him during our season together. Thank God for each of the miracles, but they are not all I need to tell you about. The real story is about what happened in both of us and how it affected us forever.

The Face of Jesus

As I have said, as I walked this challenging road with Chandan, my initial distaste and reluctance to interact with him was conquered by a barrage of Christ's love, which poured itself all over me. Chandan's presence in my life gave me the opportunity to see how repulsive my initial attitudes toward him would have been to God, and should have been to me. Instead of well-deserved condemnation, God reached down, and showered me with mercy. He helped me to exchange my old attitudes for simple, sincere Christ-like compassion. As God drew me closer to Chandan, He also drew me into a journey of new, deeper intimacy with Him. I learned that we must never think we have arrived. We are all still on the journey. With each step along the way, there is so much more wisdom and compassion available to us. Here I was, after years in ministry, still walking in so many old attitudes. This relationship with Chandan was to be my challenge. After all this time serving the Lord, was I truly growing more like Christ? Was I looking like, thinking like and loving like Jesus? Or, was my Christian walk just a religious charade in a religious parade? I confess that Chandan remained no small challenge, but I felt and valued the compelling love of God for him that grew inside of me. It was this love that gave me what I would otherwise have lacked to see that season through. God's love in my heart took direct aim at Chandan. I was launched along with it, toward him. I was dispatched into a season of compassion and appreciation for this particular divine appointment, and for this particular child of God.

Have you ever looked into the face of God? With time, I began to see the face of Jesus in the face of Chandan. It was a deeply reflective experience. I came to lose some of that hardness that each of us has as part of our inborn sinful makeup, especially those of us who are professional, self-assured (and all too often prideful) ministers. The experience was humbling. It was a beautiful gift.

Some of the people God gives us to love and care for, to nurture and disciple will never be our buddies or close friends. Many of them will be people with whom we will not have lifelong contact. These relationships may even seem burdensome and unwelcome. Nevertheless, we must understand that they are priceless gifts from God. He knows exactly what we need and how able we are to meet others at their points of need. Both Chandan and I were profoundly and supernaturally changed by our times together. I cannot speak for him, but I know the process continually squeezed away at the hardness of my heart. It destroyed much of my narrow, self-centered preconceptions and quickness to judge, which for years had been nurtured by my own pride. These times with Chandan and the experiences I had with him caused me to plumb the depths of Matthew 25:35-40.

> *(Matthew 25:35-40 NKJV) "'for I was hungry and you gave Me food; I was thirsty and you gave Me drink; I was a stranger and you took Me in; {36} 'I was naked and you clothed Me; I was sick and you visited Me; I was in prison and you came to Me.' {37} Then the righteous will answer Him, saying, 'Lord, when did we see You hungry and feed You, or thirsty and give You drink? {38} When did we see You a stranger and take You in, or naked and clothe You? {39} Or when did we see You sick, or in prison, and come to You?' {40} And the King will answer and say to them, 'Assuredly, I say to you, inasmuch as you did it to one of the least of these My brethren, you did it to Me.'"*

Mentoring Lessons from my Encounter with Chandan

1. Never displace mercy with judgment. Judgment belongs to God alone. Only His mercy belongs in us.

One of the great tests of leadership is whether we will reject the temptation to judge and embrace the demand to love. The boundless beauty of God's creation rests within every soul we encounter. Each person we mentor is irreplaceable. God provides all of them with distinctive, unique plans for their lives. They are part of His plan for ours. Our task as mentors will be to help them strip away the darkness they have experienced and endured. Underneath their sorrows, rests a potential to erupt into a joyful celebration of Christ in their lives. Let there be a flood of life-giving light. Let your light shine!

> *(Matthew 5:16 NKJV) "Let your light so shine before men, that they may see your good works and glorify your Father in heaven."*

2. Communion with the unlovely is communion with Christ.

(Matthew 25:35a NKJV) "for I was hungry and you gave Me food; I was thirsty and you gave Me drink;"

As Christ invites us to the communion table, its location and form may often surprise us. (For me, the table was often in the small sandwich shop across the street from the library.) It is clear that the banqueting table and the feast it holds are entirely the Lord's. Though we may freely invite others and partake, He remains the Host. I am convinced that the body of New Testament Scripture rejects any notion that we are authorized to limit who may partake, or even where they may partake of the communion feast. If this goes against your doctrine, I invite you to take a fresh look. It is a "*whosoever*" feast. We must never make the mistake of trying to write the guest list ourselves. Compassion clearly sets the communion table where and with whom it will. Compassion clearly serves the food and pours the drink.

(John 3:16 King James Version) "For God so loved the world, that he gave his only begotten Son, that whosoever believeth in him should not perish, but have everlasting life."

Never make the mistake of trying to write the guest list to the communion table.

---

3. Never underestimate the power of inconvenient love.

(Matthew 25:35b-36 NKJV) "I was a stranger and you took Me in; {36} I was naked and you clothed Me; I was sick and you visited Me; I was in prison and you came to Me."

Matthew's Scriptures teach us that God's kind of love is often a labor of inconvenience. Experience has taught me that it is seldom easy. On many occasions, compassion forced me to set aside my preferences and agendas. I had to reject the temptation to take the easy path, or to mutter some off-hand cliché that had little or no substance. Our words of caring and compassion become authentic when love's demands prove themselves in those most inconvenient and troubling moments - the times when we encounter the unlovely and willingly take action. On these occasions, the power of inconvenient love reveals the immeasurable vastness of the heart of the Savior, in all its power, available to work in us. These are times that stretch the heart. Yes, it will be painful to get our hearts stretched. You can count on it. Ask yourself these questions.

- Will your love be found to be only a love of convenient words and actions without meaning, void of Christ?
- Will you choose to have a ministry comfort zone of convenience? It is easy to reject God's draw to mentor certain people. We can never get very far from that built-in discomfort and distaste for the unlovely. Scripture never defines love or ministry as convenient. Both are clearly characterized as quite the opposite.

- Will your encounters with the unlovely take you deeper into love's passions? Or, will these encounters harden your heart because you choose to reject them and the opportunities they hold? We so easily disguise the hardness of our hearts with high sounding religion.
- Have you considered the power of inconvenient love to work miracles? It is an amazing tool in the hand of our amazing God. We must never underestimate that power, working in anyone, especially in ourselves!

  Again, *(1 Corinthians 13:8a NKJV) "Love never fails."*

4. Love for the unlovely becomes real when we take our hearts to the cross.

A tender heart is a crucified heart, a heart that sacrifices itself daily for the sake of others. Christ-like love grows out of such a heart. How willingly will you take your trips to the cross? If you let them, you can expect them to be daily experiences. A crucified heart will mentor wisely and well because it is ruled by love. It will bear much fruit, bring Him much glory, and will open a door for God to invade your mentoring journey with a visitation from on high. He will visit you through the unlovely, and it will be an energizing, life-giving experience to your spirit. Seize the opportunity. Take your heart to the cross.

(Galatians 2:20 NKJV) "I have been crucified with Christ; it is no longer I who live, but Christ lives in me; and the life which I now live in the flesh I live by faith in the Son of God, who loved me and gave Himself for me."

(Luke 9:23 NKJV) "Then He said to them all, "If anyone desires to come after Me, let him deny himself, and take up his cross daily, and follow Me.""

5. You will find the loveliness of God in those the world calls unlovely.

(Matthew 25:37-38 NKJV) "...Lord, when did we see You hungry and feed You, or thirsty and give You drink? {38} 'When did we see You a stranger and take You in, or naked and clothe You?"

As I have said, people are purposefully given to us as gifts from God. His gifts do not always come to us packaged in the ways we would like to have them. To the contrary, they may come to us wrapped in ways that make them appear to be void of anything we would find desirable. All we may sense is our own distaste. All we may feel is the cold darkness from within our own hardened hearts. Our perception is so darkened we cannot see the beauty of the gift, or the Giver in the gift. However, when God gives us those who seem so unlovely, then that moment becomes our opportunity to cry, *Lord open my eyes. Help me to see who You see.* When you get the opportunity, recognize it. Cry out to God over that precious one He has graced you with; and then cry over your own darkened eyes and heart. In those moments, the Spirit of God will respond to your cry. Look for Jesus in the unlovely and you will find Him. Find Him in them and you will find Him in yourself. There is no greater gift. I promise you, there will no longer be a sense of distaste in you, for you will have tasted of the sweetness of the Lord in those seemingly unlovely, unlikely souls, those precious ones only He could give you.

6. Whatever you do to the least of them will be done to God Himself.

(Matthew 25:40 NKJV) "'And the King will answer and say to them, Assuredly, I say to you, inasmuch as you did it to one of the least of these My brethren, you did it to Me.'"

There is no higher happening than finding Christ in the unlovely whom you are willing to touch. There is a powerful impact on you when Christ touches you through them. They will always be there, those we struggle to love - the inconvenient, the offensive, and even the repulsive. Jesus touched the lepers and the unclean, the outcasts and the sinners. He loved them all. His life and His words teach us a lesson worth learning - the more we press through the inconvenience and distaste of loving the unlovely, the more He will speak to us. The more He will speak to us, the more we will change and grow.

Wouldn't it be wonderful to see people just as He sees them, to touch people just as He touched them and to influence people just as He did? We all have a long way to go, but we can make the journey with Him, and with them. We have the potential to commune with Him face to face, through the faces of those beautifully unlovely ones He gives us, as we touch them with His kind of love.

Mentoring: The process of communion with Christ through the exercise of inconvenient love

(Luke 6:45 NKJV) "A good man out of the good treasure of his heart brings forth good; and an evil man out of the evil treasure of his heart brings forth evil. For out of the abundance of the heart his mouth speaks."

The words we speak can be our most effective tool for ministry. They can also be our downfall because they will reveal our hearts to those we speak to. It is so easy to say things that are shallow, off-hand clichés, but they will be empty professions of even emptier love, having no real substance to them. These are nothing more than lightly spoken lies. They are words that counterfeit the love of Christ. I have found they are quick to surface in the voices and actions of every one of us, and in our ministries. Even as we speak, we know in our hearts that what we have said is not genuine. Unfortunately, we have practiced and know this shallow communication system all too well, and are very good at working it. This often gives us an easy escape from our responsibility and accountability to love. Have you ever asked someone how they were doing, while not really caring or even listening to their answer? I certainly have. Far too often that is how we greet people. We decline to take the time or trouble. We choose not to risk exposure to what love might do. False and shallow expressions of concern will always lurk just below the surface in any conversation. Watch for them. They are quick, carnal cover-ups for a lack of caring and compassion. They conveniently hide our irritations and self-imposed limitations. They must not be in the heart of a mentor.

(1 John 3:18 NKJV) "My little children, let us not love in word or in tongue, but in deed and in truth."

Genuine love demands we go beyond uncaring, high-sounding words and the equally shallow deeds that accompany them. God's love in us only becomes authentic when it penetrates through our walls of selfishness or self-preservation. In those crucial, inconvenient moments when we encounter the unlovely, God wants to move in us to reveal love's power. Let Him do so. You will see the immeasurable vastness of the heart of the Savior. Make no mistake about it. Your heart will be stretched by inconvenient love. Yes, it can be painful to get your heart stretched, but what a valuable time it can be. I would invite you to ask yourself, Will your heart pass the test of welcoming God's love for the unlovely into it? Or, will you be found only speaking those convenient, shallow words that have no eternal meaning, words devoid of Christ? The challenge is compelling, demanding and often difficult, but with God, it is possible. We must never underestimate the power of inconvenient love to work miracles in anyone, especially in ourselves!

The Unlikely

ꕤ Todd ꕤ

It was our usual custom, in all of our churches, to spend time together fellowshipping immediately following the Sunday morning service. We understood the universal value of building relationships. People would stay around to talk, eat and enjoy the time together. Food is a common denominator that brings people together all around the world. It drew people to the church. Todd's[18] first visit was to one of these times of fellowship after the service was over. He was reluctant to sit

[18] The name has been changed.

in a Sunday service those first few weeks so he continued to show up after the service. After a few weeks of attending the after-service fellowships, Todd felt comfortable enough to come to the regular Sunday service. At the conclusion of the message that week, he answered the altar call and gave his life to Jesus.

The Word of God teaches that every sin offends God. However, each of us, because of our backgrounds and experiences, finds particular sins more distasteful than others. Todd was a man who struggled with a sin for which I had a strong aversion. When I first had occasion to minister to Todd, there was not much compassion in my heart. I carried little expectation that he would be open to my ministry, or that what I said would bring any change. Looking back, three things now occur to me. First, I am ashamed that I put such limits on myself, having had no faith for what God could do. Second, I have sorrow in my heart because my ability to see people as Jesus saw them was so limited. Third, I will always be eternally grateful for the gift of Todd in my life. My experiences with him and the ultimate opportunities I was given to be his pastor and mentor were to become meaningfully teachable moments in my ministry career and life. Todd's presence gave me another opportunity to grow to be just a little more like Jesus. My experiences with Todd changed my life and raised the level of my understanding of God's loving compassion. Once more, I saw how the Lord was willing to reach out to people just where they were, because He is in the business of redemption.

Todd soon became a regular at church. He never missed an opportunity for prayer. Every time we had a prayer meeting he sought prayer for himself. Every time the service ended he came to the altar for prayer. Whenever I spoke with him on the phone or visited him, he asked for prayer. It was not a question of his being self-centered. It was just that he had a clear awareness of how much he needed God's touch. He had much to overcome. He was hungry for God. He knew he needed the Lord just to make it through every day. Through his prayer requests and the conversations that often followed, I began to learn a great deal about him. It did not take me long to recognize his sensitivity. He was easily besieged with the issues of his life, but it was apparent that He was even more easily overwhelmed with the presence of God. During worship times in our services, he would often be on his knees, totally lost in God. In those times I prayed for him, he consistently was overcome with the moment.

Todd continued to struggle with his life, and with the temptations that accompanied it. As strong as this obstacle was, it never seemed to stop him from doing all he could to move closer to God. It became obvious that he was powerfully drawn to God. It was as if the attraction was almost magnetic. God continued to call to Todd, to draw him near. It was equally obvious that Todd had drawn a personal line in the sand between himself and the lure of the sin. He had made a choice. He would not revisit his past. He would do his best to be pleasing to God.

As the weeks and months went by, and as my heart began to soften toward him, I no longer considered it a burden or effort to pray so often for him. My prayers were transformed into words of sincere, heart-felt encouragement. They were filled with my new-found compassion for him. I watched as God began to answer. It was like the scales of judgment and prejudice I first felt toward him were being peeled away from my heart.

I began to visit Todd in town at his business. Soon he was actively seeking more than just my prayers. Now, just like Daniel (Chapter 5) he began to ask my advice. He was determined to learn how to take a godly approach to his business. I recognized that this opportunity to advise him was a vehicle through which I could personally mentor him in the ways of a godly man. Such a man would seek the Lord and include Him in life's daily decisions. This was a critical time. I knew how important it was for my advice to correspond to Scripture. I was in the midst of a God-given opportunity. Todd was receptive and accepted whatever I told him. I understood that my relationship with him, and my responses to his questions had within them seeds of success, which God could use for his sanctification and transformation. I knew it was going to be a challenge from which I could not shrink. There was too much at stake. I charged headlong into grace.

Many years have passed since we first met. He keeps me informed about how things are going for him. He is still faithfully walking with God. His life is immersed in prayer and fellowship in the church. He is a bold witness for Jesus. It is satisfying for me to see all this progress in him. I do not know what the future holds for Todd, but I know how serious he is about following Christ. He is doing his best and I am sure God will do the rest.

The beautiful thing about Todd's transformation is how it has made a difference in his family. Because of Todd's witness to them and his prayers, they received Jesus as Lord and Savior. As I reflect on the miracle God wrought in Todd's family, I can only thank God for what He did in Todd. His family now has a very different testimony than they would have if Todd had not sought the Lord so diligently. I am grateful that I could look past my prejudices and allow compassionate love to have its way in me. It opened the door for what occurred in Todd, and God subsequently opened a door through him for the rest of his family.

Mentoring Lessons from my Encounter with Todd

1. Never allow your aversion to a particular sin control your attitude toward the sinner.

The process of mentoring is a matter of self-discipline and self-sacrifice. It will take an effort to go beyond your feelings, but I have found this to be the only way to break through to the place where you can help someone to learn, grow and move ahead to become all God wants them to be.

2. Compassion is never an excuse to tolerate sin.

Compassion is to be a strong motivation to help others reject sin and embrace holiness. Scripture never teaches tolerance toward sin. Compassion always calls us to help others escape the sin. To tolerate sin is to be in agreement with it, and to serve its purposes. We have a greater purpose, to agree with, and serve our loving compassionate Savior. We are to participate with Him in bringing freedom to those captivated by sin.

(Luke 4:18-19 NKJV) "The Spirit of the LORD is upon Me, Because He has anointed Me To preach the gospel to the poor; He has sent Me to heal the brokenhearted, To proclaim liberty to the captives And recovery of sight to the blind, To set at liberty those who are oppressed; {19} To proclaim the acceptable year of the LORD."

As people struggle with temptation, they sometimes ask if it would be all right to succumb to their desires and then ask God to forgive them. It may be a naïve question, but it is something that needs to be sorted out on the spot. Our hearts must go out to them as they face the difficulties of walking in holiness, but we must be firm in our reply, "absolutely not." We must make it clear that there is no turning back from our commitment to Christ. God is with us all the way. Encourage them to press into God. In doing so, they will be able to resist the temptation. Assure them that God is changing them more every day. Be there for them for prayer and support.

3. It is your obligation to look beyond your distaste for the sin and have compassion for the person caught in it.

Compassion sees with God's eyes, feels with God's heart and loves with God's love. Compassion helped me see Todd through the eyes of love. I discovered the Jesus in him through what I saw, and it led me to have just a little bit more of Jesus in me.

(John 13:34-35 NKJV) "A new commandment I give to you, that you love one another; as I have loved you, that you also love one another. {35} By this all will know that you are My disciples, if you have love for one another."

Mentoring: The deliberate application of contagious, Christ-like compassion

Review: Mentoring Lessons from our Two Examples

1. Never displace mercy with judgment. Judgment belongs to God alone. Only His mercy belongs in us.
2. Communion with the unlovely is communion with Christ.
3. Never underestimate the power of inconvenient love.

4. Love for the unlovely becomes real when we take our hearts to the cross.
5. You will find the loveliness of God in those the world calls unlovely.
6. Whatever you do to the least of them will be done to God Himself.
7. Never allow your aversion to a particular sin control your attitude toward the sinner.
8. Compassion is never an excuse to tolerate sin.
9. It is your obligation to look beyond your distaste for the sin and have compassion for the person caught in it.

It would be wonderful to see people just as Christ sees them. Then, we could touch them and influence them just as He does. We all have a long way to go, but we can make the journey with Him… and with them. We have the potential to commune with Christ face to face, through the faces of those beautifully unlovely and unlikely ones He gives us, as we touch them with His kind of love.

What is Mentoring?

(From the definitions given in the pages of this chapter, above)

Mentoring is the intentional application of contagious, Christ-like compassion. It is a deliberate course of action in which we become God's gifts to each other. In this exchange, we open the door to communion with Christ through the exercise of our love, no matter how inconvenient it may be.

Chapter 8

A Mentor's Guide to Survival

(Romans 8:28 NKJV) "And we know that all things work together for good to those who love God, to those who are the called according to His purpose."

Consider the following questions for your ministry. First, how will you handle the disappointments that will inevitably come your way? Second, what will you do when you encounter the pitfalls that await you in your service to the Lord? Even Jesus, with His perfection and divinely ordered ministry, suffered many disappointments and had to navigate through His share of pitfalls. People turned their backs on Him on more than one occasion. One of His twelve prize pupils, Judas Iscariot, sold Him to His enemies for a price and then betrayed Him with a kiss. The rest of His disciples, and even those who were His closest friends, deserted Him at the cross. Do you believe Romans 8:28, that tells us, *"all things work together for good to those who love God and are called according to His purposes"*? Then you should be encouraged in those times you experience your own disappointments and pitfalls. God will use them to bring about something good and purposeful. Let's consider the disappointments and pitfalls every one of us will face and see what can be learned. How will you handle the disappointments?

ꕥ The Man who was a Puzzle ꕥ

Pornography knows no cultural barriers. We have encountered its affects on people around the world. One such person was Kumar,[19] a gentle, kind young man. He and his family were long-time church goers and professed a great love and commitment to Jesus. However, there was a deep-seated problem. It became clear that he was firmly captive to pornography. It was his constant temptation. He was eaten up with guilt; and the pornography was destroying his ability to live a victorious life. I genuinely liked Kumar and decided to commit whatever it took to help him overcome this devastating behavior. I had seen the vicious strangle hold pornography had on its victims. I knew that if there would be any victory for Kumar I would have to figure out how to help him free himself and put the pieces of his life back together properly. I would have to find the answer to the puzzle - how did a young man who had such a strong knowledge of the Bible and an equally strong profession of love for God become so captured by this evil?

I blocked out time for Kumar in my schedule. I met with him every few weeks. During those times we built our relationship and talked of things man-to-man. I knew Kumar was miserable in this the trap he had made for himself. He readily admitted to his shame, and for short times, he seemed to be trying hard to escape. I watched him as he struggled, making progress for a while, and then falling again. I did all I could to encourage him, to hold him as accountable as I could, but in the end, I knew I was up against a brick wall. It was a wall only Kumar could break down, but he refused to act on my counsel. The

[19] His name has been changed.

pornography remained in his life. Often the people we mentor are the only ones who can break down their walls.

Often the people we mentor are the only ones who can break down their own walls.

Kumar could not find the strength and determination to overcome. He said he loved God, but it takes more than loving God. Something was missing. (Often, in these kinds of situations, the major barrier to victory is lack of *"the fear of the Lord."*) His temptation was readily accessible wherever he went. It had given birth to sin and the sin was driving him to a place of captivity from which he could not escape.

> *(Proverbs 16:6 NKJV) "In mercy and truth Atonement is provided for iniquity; And by the fear of the LORD one departs from evil."*

It was a sad day when I finally accepted there was nothing I could do to help him change. It was time to back off on the energy and effort I was spending on him. I continued to care about him as his pastor, but I reordered my priorities and moved on to others who wanted my time. It is important to understand that we have limits to our time and energy. When you spend your time where there can be no fruitfulness, it keeps you from being effective where and when it would count for others.

Spending yourself where there is no fruitfulness will keep you from being effective where and when it counts.

Mentoring: A measured process or course of action - Will they embrace your efforts and show fruit in theirs?

Mentoring Lessons from my Encounter with Kumar

1. In the final analysis, only the people you mentor can break down their personal walls and barriers.

Determination and personal accountability will be the deciding factors in the success or failure of anyone going through the mentoring experience. The people you mentor must be determined to submit to the experience, and therefore to you if they are to change and grow. Instill in them a strong sense of accountability, first, to God, then to you as mentor. Then, challenge them to do what is necessary to bring positive change so they can achieve their destinies, hopes and dreams. You cannot do this for them. The most you can expect is to model the right attitudes and actions, holding them accountable to do the same, so they can glean from your example. I tried to do this with Kumar. He never broke through because he would not exchange those things that defined and determined his barriers for what would have set him free.

Ultimately, we will find that we are relegated to being cheerleaders for people like Kumar. The determination needed for them to embrace the mentoring process is a completely personal, internally generated one. They must renew it for themselves every day. Some days will require more of them than other days. Submission is never easy, and often requires a painful battle within, but this is a vital part of the growth process.

2. Not all of your efforts will be effective and fruitful.

Invest your time and energy where you believe it will be effective and fruitful. Effectiveness is fairly easy to define, but fruitfulness is a little more complicated. Consider how you would define fruitfulness. I encourage you to go beyond defining it simply by what you see in a person's performance and potential for achievement. Look to the intangible value of compassion released through one-to-one encouragement, especially for someone who knows their failures and expects to be rejected. I will leave it up to you to integrate these issues into your definition of fruitfulness. My hope is that you will pause and reflect on what I have just said. It may help your definition of effectiveness and fruitfulness to take on a broader meaning.

Life has its ups and downs. The trick is to keep on going, without allowing discouragement to stop you. Learn from both your ups and your downs. They are great teachers. If you will, it will better equip you for each successive battle.

The challenge is to choose wisely who we commit to, and do our best not to be deceived. This requires us to look into their hearts (and ours) at every opportunity and make the best judgments we can about them. Look for integrity in the little things. Integrity or a lack of it will not take long to surface. Little things have a way of magnifying themselves to reveal bigger things. A successful mentoring relationship requires a threefold commitment from those we mentor. The first must be from the student or disciple to the mentor. Then, look for their commitment to the mentoring process itself. Finally, look for their commitment to personal change and growth. Should you discover any of these lacking, take a serious look at the degree of commitment you ought to make to them. You will have a pretty good way of judging when to press ahead and when to back off.

It is all too easy to get wrapped up in what we are doing and not look carefully or deeply enough at what is going on inside those we are mentoring. We care so much about them that we are tempted to overlook some of the negatives as they surface. We want so strongly to see them succeed. Try not to fool yourself. Guard against looking past the negatives and recognize them for what they are. You may still be able to help them get past their negatives. With some people, the same negatives that seem to be holding them back can be turned into fertile ground for positive change. In others, the negatives become the burying ground for the person's potential. If you can help them grow past their negatives, great. It may just take a little grace and a lot of patience. Do your best to make good, timely decisions about your commitments.

3. Leave room for the grace of God to work.

Mentoring is the business of facilitating another person's process of self-discovery. God uses this process to transform them into what He wants them to be. Leave room in the process for Him to work and leave room for grace within yourself. It is not possible to know all the reasons why God appoints us to mentor a particular person, or know why he or she seems to be unwilling or unable to respond appropriately to our efforts. Some reasons will reveal themselves and others will never be revealed to us. In some cases, only when they have left our sphere of influence will the reasons manifest. Be content with not knowing, when you cannot know. I cannot tell you why Kumar did not make the trip to his freedom. I can tell you I did my best and then had to release Kumar to God. Having done your best, do not assume blame for their failures, or accept accolades for their successes. Just continue to allow God to direct your steps.

Mentoring: The business of facilitating another person's development and self-discovery

What will you do with the Pitfalls?

The mentoring experience will leave you with a lifetime of great memories. However, mixed among your memories will be decisions you made you wish you could have changed or avoided. As you look back on the challenges and sudden pitfalls that you faced, there will be regrets for what you might have done differently. In this imperfect, fallen world we cannot always make perfect choices. Regrets are normal and can be useful reminders to help us grow through our experiences. Regrets indicate we have gained a proper understanding and perspective of what is right and good (and conversely, wrong and not good). Guard yourself against feelings of guilt or even shame for what may adversely result from your good and honorable intentions. Outcomes are not always as we wish. Just keep listening to God and do your best.

(Romans 8:1 NKJV) "There is therefore now no condemnation to those who are in Christ Jesus, who do not walk according to the flesh, but according to the Spirit."

I would like to share with you principles to help you avoid two potentially fatal pitfalls common to leadership and the mentoring process. I have fallen into these pitfalls and have found that though not pleasant, they are survivable. They can even be turned into something good for the future as we move beyond them. First, seek to understand and profit from wrong decisions made because of clouded judgment; and second, refuse to allow the bad results of misplaced trust keep you from trusting again.

Judgment - Good or Clouded?

(Psalms 119:66 NKJV) "Teach me good judgment and knowledge, For I believe Your commandments."

Good judgment means forming opinions objectively or wisely, using good sense and clear, accurate discernment. Clouded judgment is the failure to do the same. It is the making of decisions or forming of opinions unwisely, ignoring the information the Lord makes available to us through our experience, senses and discernment. Hopefully, the great majority of your judgments will be good ones, but there will be times when your judgment fails, because you do not clearly see and understand the situation. To avoid clouded judgments, it is vital that you understand both the process and value of making good ones.

As leaders, our daily decisions dictate the paths we travel and influence the paths of those who travel with us. Keep in mind, we are not infallible and even with the best of intentions, we will still make our share of mistakes. Walking in the will of God is not a straight line. It wavers with the judgments we make, but we can be sure of two things. Honorable, righteous intentions will generally keep us pointed in the right direction; and, God recognizes our intentions and faithfully helps us straighten our paths. I would like to share with you six suggestions for safeguarding your successes in the mentoring process.

1. Let Scriptural truth be the deciding factor in every judgment you make. Try to make this a habit that becomes second nature to you.
2. Never be in a hurry, and never submit to pressure in making your decisions. This was taught to me early on by those who mentored me. Patient resistance to pressure has never let me down when I allowed it a prominent place in the decisions I made. Patience leaves room for God to work.
3. Listen closely to your heart. What you will hear will be the voice of the Holy Spirit who indwells you. His voice will never lie to you. Do not let your emotions, your compassion or your hopes for someone cloud what God clearly says to your heart.
4. Discern the spirits behind the people who provide you with information that you may want to use to make your decisions.
5. Recognize the people that God provides to give you wise, trustworthy and faithful counsel. Seek them out. Ask for and trust their counsel. Make it your habit to draw on their integrity and wisdom. Let them be sounding boards for your major decisions.
6. Be accountable to someone who is spiritually mature and honorable, and has a heart to watch for your soul. No one can go it alone. To do so is a sure formula for failure. God has not called you to fail. If you do your best, He will do the rest.

Misplaced Trust and Trusting Again

In this second category, we have the best of intentions and do our mentoring well, but find some individuals still let us down. We find out too late that it was a mistake to put our trust in them. This is often a surprise because there may be no outward or recognizable signs this will happen. We are let down because of character flaws that were well enough hidden to fool us. There is no shame in this. From time to time it will happen to anyone who believes in people.

I have learned to exercise great care to avoid moving people up the leadership ladder too quickly, or of placing them where they do not fit and function properly. Do everyone a favor, including yourself, and allow those you lead to have an adequate season to find their place and prove their faithfulness. Be patient, and expect the same from those you mentor. Patience is a great challenge for all of us, but especially, newly emerging leadership. There is a commendable excitement in them for ministry, and they are rightly motivated to do what is in their hearts and want to move ahead. Time always has a way of providing the tests that reveal what is in a person's heart. Your opportunity as a mentor is to facilitate the kinds of experiences they will need to climb the leadership ladder patiently and successfully.

Wrongly or prematurely promoting someone will damage them and harm those they are assigned to care for and minister to. This is not necessarily their fault. It may be they simply reach the ceilings of their abilities or competence. It may also be that they have wrongly been placed in areas of ministry they are not gifted for, and should not be functioning in. Below are five keys you should utilize to avoid premature promotions or wrongful placements.

1. Get to know your people as well as you can. There are no substitutes for investing yourself and your time in your people.
2. Discover their gifts. This will require you to find creative ways to expose them to the right opportunities, and then watch them as they begin to function in them.
3. Be observant of their weaknesses. Observe their limits. These do not indicate something is wrong. They simply acknowledge that people have God-given boundaries within which they can succeed where they are gifted and called.
4. Care about them far beyond their potential to fill whatever ministry

needs might be there. See the value in them as people to love and be with, not just as tools to be used.

5. Try not to overlook the obvious or let yourself be fooled. Wisdom is both a great teacher and a careful guardian. Utilize it.

These are sound suggestions that will help you place people properly so they can flourish, be fruitful and grow in God, right where they are. These five keys will also help you avoid having to clean up what could become a messy situation.

As we have seen, a successful mentor needs a great deal of discernment. It is far better to see the potential for failure hiding beneath the surface early, than to have to deal with it when it is exposed later. Of the five suggestions, above, the first is the most critical. Get to know your people as well as you can. Here are three sometimes well-hidden indicators of potential failure you should look for. They are sure signs of impending trouble and cannot be ignored.

First Indictor - Poor Quality of Character

I have heard it said that someone's ministry gifts will take him many places, but only his character will keep him there. A person whose character proves to be of good quality has the makings of a leader who will succeed. When you see less than honorable character, it will wave a warning like a red flag. Poor character indicates something is not right and it is time to reassess who you are dealing with. Do not ignore this warning. There are some critical character traits you should expect and in fact, demand of those you train. Consider these.

- Honesty and Honor

  Honesty may be defined as freedom from fraudulent intentions or deceitful behavior. Honor is basically honesty's twin. The two terms are synonymous. When we honor a person, we acknowledge their integrity, wholeness and trustworthy example. Honor and honesty are completely intertwined in one another (as are dishonesty and dishonor). They cannot be separated. They will clearly display themselves. There is no acceptable compromise. Either side of these qualities will show up in the little things. Given enough time, the little things grow into bigger things. So, be watchful. With a little time, a person's actions and words will paint the picture with clarity. Look carefully below, at the Apostle Paul's instructions to Timothy. They will help you understand what you are faced with as a leader, and correctly evaluate the character of those you mentor.

(2 Timothy 2:20-23 NKJV) "But in a great house there are not only vessels of gold and silver, but also of wood and clay, some for honor and some for dishonor. {21} Therefore if anyone cleanses himself from the latter, he will be a vessel for honor, sanctified and useful for the Master, prepared for every good work. {22} Flee also youthful lusts; but pursue righteousness, faith, love, peace with those who call on the Lord out of a pure heart. {23} But avoid foolish and ignorant disputes, knowing that they generate strife."

Paul's point is that both honorable and dishonorable people find their ways into the house of the Lord. He says God is looking for vessels of honor. His instructions to Timothy teach that when people repent and cleanse themselves from dishonor (and dishonesty), turning to a path of honor, they are sanctified and useful to God. Your challenge will be to find those who walk a path of honor. Find them and you will have winners and champions for Jesus.

- Commitment

Commitment is the decision to embrace and sustain a pledge or obligation to a person, a cause, a task, or way of life. Look for people who will honestly honor their commitments. These commitments must ultimately be of faithfulness to the mentor and to a lifestyle of faith toward God. It is all about having the resolve to stay the course, steadily honoring their commitments. When disappointment comes, and it will, because of someone you trained who failed their commitments, only faith in God will sustain you and help you to move ahead. The lesson for all of us is to keep our eyes on Jesus, through every success or failure.

- Faithfulness

Faithfulness is measured by the dependability a person demonstrates over a sustained period of time. Reputations for faithfulness are not easily or quickly made, but they can be destroyed in an instant of foolishness. Faithfulness describes someone who can be counted on, who is honest, honorable and committed. I have always believed that faithfulness cannot be overlooked. It is a vital indicator for recognizing potential leaders. Unquestionably, the people we are looking for are those who would "honor and commit" to be faithful.

- Work Ethic

An ethic is a set of moral principles, values and rules of conduct. A person's work ethic will showcase his character for everyone to see. Actions really do speak louder than words. Our conduct will either validate or invalidate our right to influence people's lives. Good work habits and godly work ethics ought to be very high on our list of priorities for those in the mentoring process. The people we are looking for are those who will honor, commit to and be faithful in the ways they perform their duties and tasks before the Lord.

- Compassion

Compassion has two elements or parts. First, it requires genuine, heart-felt feelings, sentiments and favorable emotions toward those who are less fortunate, perplexed or troubled. Its second part is an ability to identify with what they are going through, coupled with a willingness to do something about it. The Good Samaritan is a fine example.

(Luke 10:33-37 NKJV) "But a certain Samaritan, as he journeyed, came where he was. And when he saw him, he had compassion. {34} So he went to him and bandaged his wounds, pouring on oil and wine; and he set him on his own animal, brought him to an inn, and took care of him. {35} On the next day, when he departed, he took out two denarii, gave them to the innkeeper, and said to him, 'Take care of him; and whatever more you spend, when I come again, I will repay you' {36} "So which of these three do you think was neighbor to him who fell among the thieves?" {37} And he said, "He who showed mercy on him." Then Jesus said to him, "Go and do likewise.""

Jesus spoke of compassion and His life perfectly modeled it for us. His heart was pierced by concern for the needy, oppressed, sick and injured. Even as He died, horribly pinned to the cross, pierced in hands and feet by cold Roman nails, He cried out in the loving compassion that continued to pierce His heart.

(Luke 23:33-34 NKJV) "And when they had come to the place called Calvary, there they crucified Him, and the criminals, one on the right hand and the other on the left. {34} Then Jesus said, "Father, forgive them, for they do not know what they do..."

Compassion is the imitation of the mercy Christ had for us. I know from my own experience that it is not always easy to have a compassionate view toward others. However, I consider it a primary requirement for leadership. If you want your mentoring efforts to be fruitful, look for disciples who are people of honor, commitment, faithfulness, having a good work ethic and are full of compassion.

By now you have seen how these character traits are interconnected and how they rely upon each other to form the complete person, fully pleasing to the Lord, and one who will not let you down. Help those under your mentoring care to discover these traits within themselves. They will be door openers of destiny and significance for them.

Second Indicator - Hidden Agendas

You can be sure that what is in a person's heart will eventually make itself known to those around them. Given enough time with people, you should have no trouble judging who has hidden self-serving agendas, and who does not. Over the years, I have watched skilled manipulators do a pretty good job of hiding their true nature. However, sooner or later, their ambitions will rise to the surface. Unfortunately, it may not happen soon enough and someone might get hurt. Hidden agendas have a way of becoming obvious. Here are two questions to ask which will help you to judge the intentions of those you mentor.

1. Are they manipulators?

Manipulation is the selfish misuse of trust and position to exploit others, to gain a personal advantage. It is the uncaring, cold mismanagement of people and their circumstances. Manipulators invariably deny God's agenda and promote their own. In spite of their best efforts to hide their manipulation, there are always signs that point to the truth. One of the first signs is the feelings others have around the person in question. People are more astute than we may think. Position yourself to recognize their feelings and win their trust so they will share them with you. In the short term, feelings may lie. In the long run, they will not. Most of the time, the feelings of others who are exposed to manipulators will agree with each other. If you have been doing your job as a leader, they will likely agree with yours too.

There are other signs you can observe that will help you identify leadership in whom you have wrongly placed your trust. Ask yourself, does the person only put genuine effort into those assignments and positions that bring them personal gain? Do other people involved with those assignments and positions end up damaged in some fashion? Do your ministry agendas consistently seem to take second place behind his or hers? Are you finding resistance to your leadership and its programs that the manipulator constantly has to explain? These are reasonably easy questions to answer. The answers will not lie.

Training people for leadership ought to include consistent times when you pray together. Corporate, verbal prayer is a wonderful tool for discovering a person's heart. The Holy Spirit will reveal hidden things that would otherwise go unnoticed while you pray with people. God will not honor false, insincere prayers from manipulators. Make praying together an indispensable, regularly programmed part of the mentoring process. This needs to include training times and, perhaps more importantly, times when those you are mentoring have been released to care for others. Manipulators will be revealed by what comes from their mouths.

(Luke 6:45 NKJV) "A good man out of the good treasure of his heart brings forth good; and an evil man out of the evil treasure of his heart brings forth evil. For out of the abundance of the heart his mouth speaks."

There is no substitute for leadership that is selfless and sacrificial in attitude and deed. If you do your job of training properly, most of those you mentor will make you proud. They will learn and grow and become all God wants them to be. You will not find them manipulating for their own purposes. Quite to the contrary, you will probably have to help them understand not to neglect themselves or their families as they pursue their ministries.

2. Are they fruitful?

The biggest payoff for successful mentoring is when the people you have trained start making their own disciples. This is a true test of mentoring success or failure. Be a fruit inspector. Look at the day-to-day fruitfulness of their ministries. Do their choices often seem to miss your intentions for them and fail to bless those they are assigned to care for? Your observations have to be good enough to determine that the kinds of disciples they make are consistent with what you tried to make of them. This requires you to engage in proper oversight, and not just release them within your ministry to do their own thing and go their own ways. Keep them accountable. Take the time and trouble to insert yourself into their ministry activities. If they balk at being accountable, or are less than transparent with you, it is a sure sign they will be a problem, as will the fruit of their labors. If, however, they welcome your inspection and input, continuing to submit to and rely on you for counsel, you have winners and champions for Jesus. As Jesus said, you will know them by their fruit. It is worth repeating. Be a fruit inspector.

(Matthew 7:16-20 NKJV) "You will know them by their fruits. Do men gather grapes from thornbushes or figs from thistles? {17} Even so, every good tree bears good fruit, but a bad tree bears bad fruit. {18} A good tree cannot bear bad fruit, nor can a bad tree bear good fruit. {19} Every tree that does not bear good fruit is cut down and thrown into the fire. {20} Therefore by their fruits you will know them.""

Third Indicator - Instabilities that Surface along the Way

ꙮ TJ - A Promising Young Man ꙮ

TJ,[20] a young person in our congregation, appeared to demonstrate everything we looked for in a potential leader. He had a genuine love for God and was faithfully part of virtually all of our church activities. He had an excellent public presence, which we first discovered in our corporate prayer meetings. TJ had an obvious gift for public speaking, and had a strong knowledge of the Bible. He was friendly, compassionate and eager to serve. We, and others in the church, were building relationships with him. I began to give him teaching duties

[20] The identity has been changed.

and with time, even allowed him to preach occasionally. He was a joy to have with us.

The time arrived when Nancy and I undertook a more personal stake in his mentoring process. As was part of our mentoring pattern, we asked TJ to come to our house weekly so we could invest additional one-on-one time with him. He responded well. We were sure by this time that he had the teachable quality we always looked for in a candidate for leadership. I felt sure he had a call on his life to one day be in full-time ministry. He confirmed this to us. He felt the same. And so, I finally invited him to become an intern. He was delighted to accept, and we began to walk down that road together. This process of internship, which was actually a deepening of the mentoring process, went well for a number of months. We gradually gave him more duties and responsibilities as we supervised his progress. All seemed to be going very well. Then, the unexpected happened. It was something we never saw coming and was a real challenge to deal with.

One day his entire attitude abruptly changed. He backed off all personal interaction with us. TJ came to us and asked to be released from his internship. Though we were taken aback by all of this, we agreed to release him. When such things happen, explanations may be due, but it is futile to try to force anyone to continue in what they have already rejected. Nevertheless, both Nancy and I now had to deal with both the situation and our feelings. My experience and my instincts told me that he would be gone very quickly. I did not know the cause of the problem, but I knew from experience we might never find out. The door was closed and we had no power to reopen it. Only he could do so, and I had no expectation he would.

I was correct in assuming the worst. He left the church. It was shortly thereafter, that we were told that he had been deeply offended by Nancy and me, and that we were not the kind of pastors he could serve. The report added to our disappointment and the hurt we already felt. It was beyond our understanding. It was a mystery.

Several years passed. One day we were contacted by TJ. Amazingly, he apologized for his behavior and asked our forgiveness. Of course, we gave it to him and prayed for him. I can honestly say that doing so was an act of will, as my feelings at the moment were trying to rise up and cause me to do otherwise. Also, I can say it took some time to overcome those feelings and understand that there were forces at work I could not know or control, and apparently neither could he. Looking back, I think we did the right thing to give him the opportunity to become an intern. I would do the same today. I will never know the details about what he was dealing with, but I do know TJ is in God's hands and He cares for him more than we ever could.

Mentoring Lessons from my Encounter with TJ

Problems may surface after you entrust someone with promotion and position. This happens in spite of having done your best to know them and having done what wisdom dictated. Some things will simply remain hidden until after you move on your instincts and promote someone. My best advice to you is to do your best, and continue to walk in faithfulness to God and to those you are entrusted with. Do not forsake those principles that got you where you are. When a problem arises, let God help you sort things out. Then take whatever action is required. Here are a few of the inherent limitations that may surface unexpectedly.

1. Personality Quirks and Instabilities

Even people with the best intentions may have personality quirks or instabilities that surface only after they are placed in leadership positions. With every promotion comes new pressures. Often, people do not even know they have a particular issue until it surfaces in the midst of the pressures. When it surfaces, everyone else may see it, but they may be blind to it.

I have learned to place a priority on finding out as much as I can about the people I mentor. It is important that you develop and maintain a good personal relationship with them. Doing so allows you to speak correction into their lives, and allows them to receive it comfortably. A good relationship is no guarantee you will see their quirks and instabilities. However, it does give you a better chance. We have had a lot of improper teaching about leaders distancing themselves from those they lead. If I read the gospels and epistles correctly, a good leader is a reachable leader, just as a good disciple is a reachable disciple.

2. Uncontrollable or Unpredictable Emotions

One thing people valued the most in my leadership was my stability and predictability. Pastoral care is all about consistency, steadiness and reliability. Peace among the flock comes from knowing the shepherd, knowing his or her ways, and relying on that knowledge for assurance and comfort. This principle is universal. It finds its way into every fellowship and works equally at every level of leadership. People want to know what to expect from their leaders. They do not want to have to worry about who we are, or what we might or might not do. If leaders are unpredictable, or even predictably unstable, people will go elsewhere seeking to be led by someone who is both predictable and able to stay under control. Make stability and predictability a measurement for your disciples.

3. Boundaries and Limitations

There will be times when you find yourself working with good, God-fearing people who desire to serve faithfully, but are approaching the edge of their boundaries and limitations. Their hearts will be right toward you and God, but eventually it becomes clear they do not fit the ministry positions that are in your heart for them, or in theirs. They try their best, but simply do not possess the call, the gifts or the natural abilities needed to function in that particular position. Your reaction will be critical to their futures. Help them to recognize the situation. Gently guide them to understand their boundaries and limitations. Encourage them to make the necessary adjustments and to discover the great opportunities God has for them. As they do, they will recognize and nurture the gifts He has given them for the direction He wants them to go.

You will find that some of those you mentor will be contained and kept back because they suffered bad experiences and hurtful circumstances. Others may have self-imposed limitations. They may not be teachable. They might previously have been subject to poor leadership or improper, inaccurate biblical teaching. Some will just be stubborn. In spite of your best efforts, these people will refuse to allow old ideas and attitudes to be challenged or changed. For reasons nobody can explain, some simply will not be able to grasp what you are trying to give them. They may not be able to understand what their proper roles, responsibilities and opportunities in ministry are. Unfortunately, you cannot always discern who these people are until later in the mentoring process. If you use wisdom, and apply some of the things I have talked about, you will minimize this. The good news is that through your willingness to commit to them, most of those you choose to mentor will be good choices and will have satisfying and successful service to the Lord.

ꕤ Three Pitfalls ꕤ

As we close the chapter, let me give you three pitfalls to watch for.

1. Putting the work of God before your relationship with God

When you put the work of God before your relationship with Him, though your intentions may be good and honorable, your priorities are skewed and out of biblical order. Others then imitate and model them, because they see them as the proper ways of ministry life. There are no substitutes for keeping God first in your life and walking in the counsel of the Scriptures. Teach this. Model it for all to see. Require it of your disciples. If you leave nothing else with them but the urgency of having intimacy with God, you will accomplish what is foremost in God's heart.

2. Praying self-serving prayers, asking God to bless your ways, even as you disregard His

Again, your intentions are good and honorable, but you are so driven by your own agenda (as good as it is), that you fail to find out what is in God's heart and adjust yourself accordingly. God's thoughts and ways do not always make sense to us, but they are inevitably better and surely able to take you to your destiny.

3. Losing sight of your purpose and drifting off course

You major in the routines instead of your divinely-authored purpose. You have become trapped in your daily habits. Because they have veered from your original divine purpose, your routines become wearisome and your life is far less fruitful than you hoped and dreamed it would be. Get yourself back on course. Consider what the Lord wants and go back to it.

There is a story told about the captain of the finest battleship in the British navy. It was during a stormy, fog-filled night. He was on the bridge of his ship when he received a short message. It read, "Danger of collision, adjust your course ten degrees to the north." He sent back a reply, "No, you adjust your course ten degrees to the south." A second message came back, "Please respond now. Adjust your course ten degrees to the north immediately." The captain rose up in all his pride and began to shout at his radio operator, "Send back another message, 'I am the captain of the greatest battleship in the Royal Navy. My course is set. You adjust yours. Move ten degrees to the south.'" Quickly the next message came, "I cannot do that. Make the adjustment now." The captain was so mad he could no longer control himself. "This is my last warning. I am the captain of a great warship. I demand you move ten degrees to the south and get out of my way. Who do you think you are?" There was a pause for a few seconds. The reply came back, "I am the keeper of the lighthouse. You really ought to rethink where you are going."

The solution to avoiding the pitfalls we just looked at is to make a course adjustment. Open your heart right now. If you see any of these pitfalls staring you in the face, obey God's Word, make that adjustment, get back on track, and keep on moving toward your destiny.

What is Mentoring?

(From the definitions given in the pages of this chapter, above)

Mentoring is a measured process or course of action in which people are challenged to embrace your efforts and show fruit in theirs. It is the business of facilitating another person's development and self-discovery.

Chapter 9

Transitions

In this chapter we will consider those times when the season of mentoring someone comes to an end. It was probably a good, satisfying time of service to the Lord and to the person you gave your heart to. It was a time when a friend was made and experiences were shared. Now you can look back and celebrate your friendship and successes. You can also ponder the things that did not quite work out as you wished, and reflect on how much your season of mentoring really cost you. You can use these reflections to better guide yourself through what is coming next. This will help you go forward with less stress, better able to handle any new surprises, and become more proficient in your servant leadership to those you touch.

I want to share some thoughts with you about two of the ways mentoring seasons end. The first is when the people you mentor finish their time with you, seize the opportunities given them, and move on to other places of service. As this happens, you have to let go of them. Your season together is at an end. In the second instance, God calls you to move on. The people you have led and mentored are left behind and now have to find their own ways. The relationships may continue at some level, but the severing of the day-to-day ties you had with them is not easy or pleasant. It becomes a real challenge to both you and them. Let's look at these two types of transitions.

First Transition: Their season ends. They move on. You have to let go.

You can no longer be a part of what they are doing. You can only rejoice in and celebrate the reports of their successes from a distance. They are gone. Now you advise and encourage them only when they allow you to… and only from a distance. Your opportunities to help them become their choice, not yours. There is likely to be a painful sense of loss within you. This is completely normal and should be expected. You have poured yourself out for them. You have loved them and they have loved you. Because mentoring is your gift and calling, you also loved the process you brought them through. Now you are left with an empty spot in your heart. This is to be expected. Let God fill it. Rejoice in what was. Look forward to what will be.

ꕥ Danny and Sheila ꕥ

I met Danny at a church planter's course. It was being held by a large, influential church in our city, as one of the ways they contributed to the spread of the Gospel. I had taken my share of church planting courses and taught the subject on more than one occasion. I was there because after the experience of our first church plant in New York City in 1999, I knew that the challenges of growing a church there would require new ways of thinking and new relationships with other like-minded people. Nancy and I were there to see what we could learn and to link up with whomever the Lord might provide. Our newly planted church was off to a good start, but we understood that all the fresh insight, training and help we could get would be invaluable. So here we were, in our first morning of the class, sitting across a conference table from Danny. It would not take long for the Lord to begin speaking to me about him

As the months passed, Danny and I got to know each other well. Danny had a lovely wife, Sheila, and beautiful family. They lived in a high rise in the city. Danny had ministered for years as an evangelist on the streets. He was just a great guy with a huge heart for God. He was in the class with us because he felt a call and urgency to plant and pastor his own church.

Nancy and I agreed that we would invite Danny and Sheila to join with us for a season. I would mentor and coach him in the skills he would need for pastoring until he and Sheila were ready to launch out on their own. They were delighted with our offer and we began our journey together. Danny was gifted and already had many of the skills required for pastoring a church. He was a willing pupil who caught on quickly. He and Sheila had hearts of compassion and zeal, which was contagious among our people. They were a blessing to the church and a wonderful asset to us. We grew to have great affection in our hearts for their family.

Then the day came when they were ready to launch out and plant their church. It would be hard to lose them. I even had a secret hope that one day Danny could take over our church. It was a good plan, but it was not God's plan. I knew I had to give Danny room to do what was in his heart, and not try to influence him to stay for my own selfish reasons. The day came when we prayed over Danny and his family and sent them out. Nancy and I did what we could to smooth the way for them. We continued to provide them with our prayers, lots of encouragement and all the financial support we could give them. Some of our people even went with them to the new church plant. I made sure Danny knew I would be there for him if he needed me.

Although we felt sadness and disappointment, we would not dwell on what might have been, could have been, or perhaps even what should have been. We comforted ourselves with the knowledge that there are no surprises in heaven and God always knows what He is doing. So Nancy and I celebrated their going and I thanked God for allowing us to help them get ready.

Mentoring Lessons from Danny and Sheila

1. Keep your heart kingdom-centered, not self-centered or even centered on others.

   Your stewardship over people will always be temporary. Knowing that the people you care for and have invested yourself in are going to leave may not always be pleasant, especially when they could fit so well with the needs for your ministry. However, it is important to maintain a broader view of what God is doing. Remind yourself, your assignment and purpose, as a mentor, is to equip people for the work of God and for Kingdom business. Be motivated and compassionate for what their futures hold beyond their times with you. Otherwise, you will delay or deny their opportunities to fulfill the will of God, to be successful and significant in His kingdom.

   (Psalms 118:24 NKJV) "This is the day the LORD has made; We will rejoice and be glad in it."

2. God is sovereign. Trust Him for the future.

   Do your best to understand God's sovereignty as it relates to what you are doing. This will help you maintain a personal conviction of unshakable trust in Him and keep things in perspective. His ways are not always understandable, but they are always good. Be sure you do not require an explanation or justification from God for the ending of the season and the loss of the people. Otherwise, you will be frustrated and prone to wrong thinking, which could lead you off course from what God has next for you. Your loss will be His gain, and ultimately, your gain… and theirs.

(Philippians 3:7-8 NKJV) "But what things were gain to me, these I have counted loss for Christ. {8} Yet indeed I also count all things loss for the excellence of the knowledge of Christ Jesus my Lord, for whom I have suffered the loss of all things, and count them as rubbish, that I may gain Christ"

Surrender to God often becomes somewhat of a fight. In these times, open your heart and get your assurance by looking to the Word of God. Remind yourself of how faithful He has been, and that your commitment to Him calls for your complete trust. This may require you to reach into your reservoir of faith and take hold of what you know and have already experienced about His faithfulness. He will not let you down.

(Isaiah 55:8-9 NKJV) "For My thoughts are not your thoughts, Nor are your ways My ways," says the LORD. {9} "For as the heavens are higher than the earth, So are My ways higher than your ways, And My thoughts than your thoughts."

(Proverbs 3:5a NKJV) "Trust in the LORD with all your heart..."

3. Celebrate them and celebrate the hand of God in their going.

Serving the Lord is all about having the right view of things. Rehearse what He has done. Declare what He is about to do. Then celebrate four things. First, celebrate the gift God placed in you that allowed you to mold the lives of those who are about to leave. Second, celebrate the gift from God of those who are leaving, full of all you gave them. Third, celebrate what God is going to allow them to do after they are gone. Finally, celebrate what God will call you to next. It may have been good, but it is going to get even better. That is the way it is in a life of obedient service to God and His people.

Second Transition: Your season ends. You move on. They have to let go… and so do you.

(Acts 20:22-24 NKJV) "And see, now I go bound in the spirit to Jerusalem, not knowing the things that will happen to me there, {23} except that the Holy Spirit testifies in every city, saying that chains and tribulations await me. {24} But none of these things move me; nor do I count my life dear to myself, so that I may finish my race with joy, and the ministry which I received from the Lord Jesus, to testify to the gospel of the grace of God."

Consider the following scenario. It is time for your new assignment, and perhaps a new location. You answer the call of God and you move on. All you have built and devoted yourself to is now finished or given to another. You have defined much of your identity by what you did, and who you did it with. Now all that is past. Again, there is that familiar empty spot deep in your heart. I have felt this every time I obeyed God and moved on. Experience has taught me that these emotions signal I had been what God wanted me to be in the season that was closing. I have also learned that God is very good at filling my heart with new people, new challenges and more of Himself, so I can become all He wants me to be in the new season at hand.

And so you move on in the will of God. Yes, you will certainly find yourself mourning for what used to be. You invested so much of yourself. You had so many good friends. You enjoyed the respect and honor you received. Now, you find yourself being a new face in a new place. Your life seemed so full just a short time ago and now has gaping holes in it. There may be too much time and not enough to do to satisfy. Or, there may be much to do, but no familiar faces to do it with. Your comfort zone has evaporated. Just like that! The difference this time is that the people you leave find their comfort zones also evaporating. Like you, your friends are face to face with the discomfort of change. Suddenly, their lives have gaping holes in them too. God has grace enough to carry them through, just as He will you.

When the transition comes, and your comfort zone has evaporated, you may find yourself questioning the nature of your own identity. You used to be the leader, the pastor, the mentor - God's man or woman of faith and power. Now, you have a brand new chapter before you and the pages are blank. Sometimes, you may even feel disconnected from God, and have a sense of powerlessness, a feeling that your faith did not make the trip with you. The thing that hurts most is that you just want to serve God and be fruitful, but it seems you are out of the loop and unable to exercise your gifts and experience. Your training and knowledge tell you it is another of those times on the Potter's wheel. You look for the Potter and it seems He is ignoring you. What could be more painful?

Having to leave what was so good has been my own experience on more than one occasion. Yes, I have been there. My guess is you have too. If not, you probably will one day. It is all part of serving the Lord. Yes, it is truly painful. Let me share with you one such experience when I transitioned to a new season.

꧁ Letting Go and Going Forward ꧂

After my bout with cancer (Chapter 4), we left New York City in 2000 to recuperate in Florida for about 18 months. In December of 2001, the Lord directed us to return to New York City to plant another church. Fast forward to the spring of 2006. We had been pastoring our new church plant for four years now. It was a multicultural, international church, full of people who were hungry for God and loving each other. It was our baby. We had labored so hard to plant and nurture it. We loved our people and it had been a wonderfully fruitful time. Now the Lord spoke to us and again, clearly said, "Go." Nancy and I both knew it was time for us to fold the tent and leave New York City for that final time. We might come back on occasion to visit or minister, but we would never live there again. Leaving New York City meant we would have to end the chapter, and start with a blank page once again. We had tried several avenues to find replacements to pastor our bilingual (English/Mandarin) church, but we could not find anyone willing to move to New York City. I could only conclude that, sadly, it was God's will to close things down and for us to move on. The Sunday came when we finished our final service, said our goodbyes and prepared to go back to our home church in Florida. Yet, again, the Lord had directed us to leave a meaningfully fruitful work. It was extremely difficult for me, but I knew that obedience to the voice of God and to His will must have precedence over my own plans, dreams and desires.

The hardest part in leaving was knowing how painful it was for the people who loved us and had come to rely upon us as their pastors. We sought comfort for ourselves by looking back to the end of our time in Fiji. We had so many reports from people there who had moved on to great things after we left. The paths their lives took helped them to understand our leaving was the will of God, not just for us, but for them too. We still receive emails and phone calls from our friends in both Fiji and in New York City, telling us how they would never have experienced what God is doing in their lives, had we not obeyed and moved on. Our leaving released them from dependence on us and kick-started them into their destinies. Though it was a great season when all of us walked together, the greater purpose was always about each person's individual walk with God. Knowing this has given us some comfort, though we will always feel the loss of those beautiful times and the closeness of those wonderful relationships. The mentoring lesson here is a simple, yet powerful one. Someone's destiny is always waiting on the other side of your obedience.

Someone's destiny is always waiting on the other side of your obedience.

Never question obedience to the voice of God. He always knows best for all concerned. My obedience to leave Fiji and go to New York City resulted in my healing. God knew just what I needed. He had doctors waiting on the other side of my obedience, who would supply my need for very special care. Their care, and God's hand restored my health. We had left Fiji without questioning. Our obedience insured that we would fulfill our destinies. We would not be stopped. As we left New York City in 2000 and drove south to Florida, I rejoiced over my healing, and was eternally grateful for His loving grace. Still, I did not want to go. When you serve God, times of disappointment and hurt are inevitable. Leaving New York City would not have been my choice. Now, six years later, we were leaving again. Each time God spoke to me to leave, it was emotionally difficult. It was just plain tough. Still, the conclusion of each act of obedience became the door to my blessings. Each led me away in great sadness, but then, to greater joy. Now my world has expanded globally and my ministry continues to reach out beyond the borders and limitations I used to have. As always, God was faithful and knew exactly what He was allowing to happen in my life. As my journey continued, there would be great gain ahead. God was taking me from genuine pain and a sense of loss to something eternally fruitful and full of potential I would otherwise never have realized.

Obedience to the voice of God is never to be questioned. He always knows best for all concerned.

(James 1:2 NKJV) "'My brethren, count it all joy when you fall into various trials,"

I have learned that when the cost seems to be overwhelming, stop counting the cost and start counting it all joy. God will not waste your pain. He will invest it for your future success and His glory. Take yourself beyond counting the cost. Remind yourself that you could never count the number of the thoughts God has toward you, and you could never find or measure the limits to His grace. He will not abandon you in your journey to serve Him. He will be there for you and will take you through to your destiny.

(Psalms 139:17-18 NKJV) "How precious also are Your thoughts to me, O God! How great is the sum of them! {18} If I should count them, they would be more in number than the sand; When I awake, I am still with You."

Mentoring: God's limitless grace infused into your obedience, affecting the destinies of those you touch

Mentoring Lessons from Seasons' Endings

1. Obedience to the voice of God must have precedence over your own feelings or desires, whatever they may be.

Obedience always demands some sort of test. Knowing it was time to obey God, and accepting change, has often been a test of my will. I have learned that God is more interested in our personal growth and eternal fruitfulness than He is in creating or allowing us comfort zones, no matter how fruitful they seem. It appears that we flourish most when our faith is challenged in the face of some kind of an uphill climb. It only makes sense. He is the ultimate Coach, trying to get us to gain the best He has for us. This requires a challenge to us, our feelings, desires, and especially, our faith.

2. God never makes a mistake. He always knows best.

The voice of doubt never changes. It will always challenge what God has said and try to convince you to disregard it. The voice of doubt formed its patterns as the serpent spoke to Eve. These patterns recurred all through the Bible. Satan even tried using doubt to tempt Jesus in the desert. In Acts, Chapter 3, the Apostles Peter and John were threatened. The Sanhedrin demanded they disobey their divine charge to preach and abandon their God-given purpose. They refused. This same voice of doubt continues today in countless places and will be with us until the Lord returns. It is an easily recognized pattern. Doubt always tries to take God off the throne. It cajoles or coerces us into putting ourselves, something, or somebody else on it. It does this by casting misgivings on both God's credibility and His sovereignty.

Our remedy is also a pattern, and it never changes either. We are to embrace our obedience, partner it with our faith, and continue with it into the future. Then, as our faith flourishes, doubt withers away and loses its voice. It may not always be easy. It may require us to fight for it.

God really does know best, all the time, every time. He is incapable of making a mistake. He is absolute in faithfulness to us, infinite in power for us, and rules over everything against us. It is not possible, given the perfection of His nature, for Him to fail. Just continue to go with Him. You will be fine.

We flourish most when our faith is challenged.

꧁ Ben ꧂

I will always count Ben as unique and precious among the people God has given me to mentor. He is the only one of all those I have mentored or pastored who became like my own brother. It started when we first came to New York City in 1999. A friend of ours had been a missionary to China and knew an old Chinese man. The only way to describe this man accurately is to say he is an honored, wise and knowing servant of the Most High. At great personal risk, he travels in and out of China, functioning in an apostolic role to the underground Chinese church. One morning, just after we had settled into our new apartment, this incredible servant of God showed up at our door. He introduced himself and let us know that he was there to offer whatever help he could. It was an unexpected surprise. By now you have learned that one of my favorite sayings is to "expect the unexpected." Another is to "anticipate the inevitable, supernatural intervention of God." I will always believe that the appearance of this man of God, knocking on our door was truly the unexpected, supernatural intervention of God. One of the things he did was to hand us money to pay our first month's rent. Another was to connect us with Ben, which was to be the beginning of a truly significant life-long relationship.

Ben had been in New York City about fifteen years. His life was not easy. He washed other people's clothes for a living. Six days a week he would pick up their clothes, take them away and wash them. Then, he would deliver them all nicely folded back to their owners in the evening. His life was typical of so many immigrants, struggling to make it in New York City.

We soon found Ben to be a gentle, good hearted, faithful friend. He had a quality few of us ever achieve. As best as I could tell, He was filled with unshakable faith. He relied completely on God for everything. This is not a cliché. I watched him. It was how he lived every moment of his life. He was one of the most humble, gentle and gracious people I have ever met. He had an incredible understanding of kingdom living. He was a servant among servants. If you want to learn how to love God, just get around Ben. By the way, he also could sing and play the guitar. He became our worship leader and ultimately, helped us in all three of our churches in New York City. He knew how to usher us into the throne room. I think that is where he lives. Our worship was a lovely thing right from the beginning. It was so unexpected. It was so pure. It was a sure sign to Nancy and me that God was with us. After all, He sent us Ben.

I could fill a book with Ben's story, but that is for another time. I will keep it brief and to the point. As the years went by, we relied on him for so much of the routine that was happening in the church. He was more than just our worship leader. He was there whenever we needed him, in whatever way we needed. He was the first to the church and the last to leave. All the logistics of setting up and tearing down the church were in his hands. Whenever we had something special going on, Ben was there, doing all he could. He was a servant, but that is not the point of what I want to say. There was so much more to him. He made it his personal responsibility to watch over us and give all he was to us without any expectation or demand of anything in return. He was as pure an example of Christ's presence in someone as I have ever known. Ben looked like, acted like, talked like and loved like Jesus. His life was a wonderful challenge to my own. I am the better for it. I learned to love him.

The day came when Ben helped load the rental van with our furniture and then Nancy and I said our final goodbye. He watched as we drove off to Florida. I am sure his heart was broken, as I know mine was. We all knew beyond a doubt it was God's will and His timing. We had to let go and so did Ben.

The story does not end there. I had recognized the pastoral gift in Ben. Over the years we were together, he had taken Bible school courses and I had trained him in pastoral ministry. Just before we left, I ordained him. About six months later, he returned to Malaysia to begin pastoring in the church he left twenty years ago, when he first came to America. Ben left New York City in obedience to God. His door was wide open. He seized the moment and walked through.

We did not know at the time, but we were destined to find ourselves with Ben in Malaysia within a year and a half of leaving New York City. We were then able to have a joyful reunion and celebrate what God was doing with him. God allowed us to see the fruit of our labor of love toward him. He was walking in the reward of his labor of love toward us, but more importantly, the reward of his labor of love toward God. It was not goodbye forever. We will be returning to Malaysia to train leaders in a Chinese Bible school at least once a year for the foreseeable future and will get to be with Ben when we are there. In fact, as I write this, we are making plans to be with Ben in a few months. Jeremiah, who you read about in the beginning of the book, will meet us there too.

> *(Hebrews 11:6 NKJV) "But without faith it is impossible to please Him, for he who comes to God must believe that He is, and that He is a rewarder of those who diligently seek Him."*

ꕤ Marilyn ꕤ

In those days in New York City, our Tuesday evening prayer meetings in Manhattan were exciting and filled with the moving of the Holy Spirit. The meetings were attracting many people from beyond our regular church family. We never knew who would come, but we marveled at how so many kept coming, hungry for a touch from God. Marilyn was among these people. She came from the South Bronx, where she had grown up in a rough, challenging neighborhood. She had gone through numerous hurts and had some deep emotional scars.

Yet, she had risen above all that and now was working very successfully as a nurse. She loved God and had established a ministry to hurting women in the Bronx, called The Potter's Lady." She was making a measurable difference in the lives of lots of women who were hurting, lonely and in need. She was an incredibly loving and faithful person. Her heart melted at the difficulties these women in her neighborhood faced. She had heard and responded to the call of God to give herself to them.

As the months went by, Nancy and I got to know her and we saw what was in her heart. We encouraged her to go deeper in God. She was going through a trying time in her own church, which was experiencing some serious leadership setbacks. She hung in with her church and its leaders for quite a while and tried her best to be a positive influence. However, she finally felt she had no choice but to end her commitment there. She came to us carrying deep hurts from that experience, and still dealing with some other personal issues from her past. By then, we had developed a strong relationship with her, and so, she came under the wing of our pastoral care. We began to do what we could to help her move ahead.

As time went by, Marilyn became a vital part of our fellowship. Nancy and I were amazed at how she bonded with the women in the church. It was especially gratifying to see the compassionate love in her, as she reached out to them. They responded in kind toward her. It was a classic case of a wounded healer making a difference among others, most of whom were also wounded. A great number of the women she touched were Chinese, and many were hurting from years of neglect or abuse. Though these women were culturally very different from this Hispanic woman from the Bronx, there were no barriers she could not breach. There are those special moments when the moving of the Holy

Spirit profoundly impresses us. I will never forget one such moment. It happened during a prayer meeting in one of our Chinese homes. Nancy and I watched Marilyn and about six of our Chinese women sitting together on the floor, arm in arm. They were holding each other and praying for each other. It was a beautifully tender moment. The love of Christ flowed like a river of healing among them. It was so thick you could almost touch it. How special it was that God brought Marilyn to us.

The day came when we invited Marilyn to become our women's pastor. This was our recognition of the hand of God working in and through her. We had seen Christ work so powerfully in her to touch those precious women in the midst of their emotional trials and trauma. In the process of their healing, she got her healing too.

Marilyn is like a daughter to us. When we left New York City she was particularly hard hit by the change. Nancy and I remain like family to her. She has a very special place in our hearts. We continue to talk by phone with her and will see her from time to time, as the occasion permits. After we left New York City she moved to a church pastored by friends of ours and became their youth pastor. It is a different challenge for her. The same compassion and love that healed her and made her such a blessing for us is providing a way for her to make a difference once again. Her zeal for God and the love within her is impacting the young people of the church she now ministers in. She continues to minister to her friends in the Potter's Lady in the South Bronx. She is moving toward her potential and the hand of God is upon her. Don't you love it when God's grace and perfect planning is revealed?

Mentoring Lessons from Ben and Marilyn

(John 15:15 NKJV) "No longer do I call you servants, for a servant does not know what his master is doing; but I have called you friends, for all things that I heard from My Father I have made known to you."

1. There are people who will challenge the depth of your walk with God because of what you see in them.

God has His ways of encouraging us with the knowledge that we can become so much closer to Him and so much more like Him. He often does this through the people we have mentored, loved and then had to let go of. Looking back, I think of Ben's constant modeling of Christ's servanthood, and Marilyn's consummate example of God's tender mercies. They both challenge me, because I can expect great things for myself as I model the Christ in Ben and Marilyn. The simple truth is, when you saw either of them, you saw Jesus. He showed Himself through the hearts of these two friends of His, who could be relied upon to display and dispense the perfect grace and lovingkindness He placed within them. Look for people like them. Embrace them as special gifts from God. Watch them and learn. It will be an education you will cherish forever.

2. Letting go is going to be painful.

Parting from good friends is difficult. It will hurt. The good thing about the hurt is that it signals the special quality of the friendships. Losing the day-to-day closeness lets you know how valuable the experience with them was. It also helps you to understand in some small, but not insignificant measure, how incredibly painful it must have been for Christ to leave His friends and turn His face toward the cross.

3. Much of the reason for parting will be revealed by the growing impact of those you loved and had to leave.

Our example again is the Lord. Resurrection Sunday brought His disciples great joy. His success could never replace their knowledge of His suffering, but it brought understanding to them of why it all happened. The celebrations that followed did not make the pain any less, but it helped them to see the greatness of God and understand how it could all be worth the sacrifice and suffering. The experience of Christ and His early followers reminds us that we serve a good God who always has a great plan. It helps us understand the changing seasons and manage the hurts of losing the comfort of our friends. When your seasons change, move ahead through the pain and loss. Gird yourself with obedience, love and faithfulness. You will be conformed even more to the image of His Son and God will be pleased.

(Romans 8:28-29 NKJV) "And we know that all things work together for good to those who love God, to those who are the called according to His purpose. {29} For whom He foreknew, He also predestined to be conformed to the image of His Son, that He might be the firstborn among many brethren."

Mentoring: The processes of learning, combined with the experiences of life, which are walked out in obedience, resulting in good people doing great things for God

In the beginning, I quoted President Ronald Reagan, *"A great leader is not a man who does great things, but a man who gets others to do great things."*

The difference you make will ultimately be measured by the differences made by the people you mentored. What you have been reading is not about me. It is about people like Danny, Ben, Marilyn and the others I have spoken of, who are great servant-leaders and great difference makers. Seeing people affecting others for Jesus is all the satisfaction any of us should look for. It can never be about me or you. It must always be about those we influence and help to change, so they can let their lights shine brightly enough to reveal the good news of Christ, the Risen Lord.

The difference you make will ultimately be measured by the differences made by the people you mentored.

(Matthew 5:14-16 NKJV) "You are the light of the world. A city that is set on a hill cannot be hidden. {15} Nor do they light a lamp and put it under a basket, but on a lampstand, and it gives light to all who are in the house. {16} Let your light so shine before men, that they may see your good works and glorify your Father in heaven."

What is Mentoring?
(From the definitions given in the pages of this chapter, above)

Mentoring is God's limitless grace, infused through your obedience, into the processes of learning and life, affecting the destinies of those you touch.

Chapter 10

Just a Little Bit More

As I look back through the previous chapters, I do so with wonder. God's grace has continually worked in my life and those around me in ways that have gone beyond our weaknesses, flaws and imperfections to bring about His perfect will.

In the previous nine chapters, the word "love" appears over two hundred times. I am fully convinced I was purposefully guided by the Holy Spirit to include so many references to love. God's kind of love (New Testament agape) is the underlying foundation of biblical mentoring. Just a little bit more of it every day creates a rock-solid basis for who we are and what we do.

God's Kind of Love

We were finishing three weeks of teaching and preaching in Malacca, Malaysia at a Chinese language Bible school. I often am asked to minister (with local interpretation) at various places in Asia. I had spent two of the weeks teaching Bible Study Methods and a third week on Leadership Training. During this time we had come to know many of the students well. It seemed to be a fruitful time and compared to the best we had experienced in short-term missions. Now it was the last evening of ministry there and I had been asked to preach an evening service in a local Chinese church. All our students would be there.

Everything went well with the sermon. At the conclusion, we worshiped and waited on the Lord. After a while, I began praying over many who were sick, others who were demon possessed and a good number who were suffering emotional scars from the past. During this time, Nancy had been sitting on the opposite side of the altar from where I was ministering. People began to spontaneously line up for her to pray over them too. God was touching His people. It must have taken us close to two hours to pray for all those who wanted prayer.

There was a student I had spent considerable time talking with during our three weeks at the Bible school. I knew he was full of promise, with a call to pastor. As we neared the end of the evening, he approached me and asked if I would lay my hands on him and impart to him the same love and compassion for people he had seen in me. I was humbled. There were many things he could have asked for that were evident in our three weeks together. Yet, he saw something that he counted more valuable than anything else he could ask for. That one thing was God's kind of love in me. I gave him a big hug, and prayed for what he asked. He fell to the floor weeping and lay there a long time. I have no doubt God answered his request. I glanced over to where Nancy was. The same love was flowing. It was an unforgettable demonstration of God's kind of love poured over all of us. It was a night I will never forget.

For the previous three weeks, we had deposited good teaching into the lives of those at the Bible school. The one thing that touched them significantly went beyond what our lessons taught. They caught the reality of God's kind of love, because they saw it in us. We were contagious with it and they caught it.

What is God's kind of love? I arrived at this definition after much reflection on the subject over many years. Notice how the definition is given in the first person. God's kind of love is always a "first person" issue. It is always about God at work inwardly in me, so He can show Himself outwardly through me.

> *God's kind of love in me, is my intentional, consistent effort to bring as much of God's grace, His presence and His provision to someone, regardless of what it costs me.*

From the definition, we see that God's kind of love is always...

- Intentional
- Consistent
- An effort
- Sacrificial

God's kind of love is deliberate, dependable, ongoing hard work. Everything about God's kind of love is intended to deliver God's grace to someone, through you. Look again at my definition of God's grace from Chapter 1.

> *Grace is all the goodness of God, the expression of His limitless, unbounding love, just waiting for you. God releases it in your time of need. It need not be earned, for it is His freely given gift. It is what you could never do for yourself and only He could do for you. It is sufficient for any circumstance. It is most often expressed through one person to another.*

Grace is the purest imitation of Christ and the most powerful demonstration of God that can be experienced. When it comes from you, you become a living display of God's kind of love, which can be explained as a transfer of divine grace. If I am going to be successful at loving those I mentor and lead, I am going to have to know, above all the other things, how to transfer something of God (specifically His love), from within me to a place within someone else.

I remember Nancy and me walking to the market place near our church in downtown Suva. Along the way there were street vendors selling juice. It was always hot and humid in Fiji and people would pause and purchase a drink from the vendor. The juice was stored in a rather large and weather-beaten plastic container that sat on a table. The person selling the juice would take a glass, dip into a smaller container of water to clean it, and then fill it with juice. When you finished your drink, you returned the glass and it was dipped again in the same container of water to prepare it for the next customer. As you can imagine, this process was less than up to the sanitary standards we were used to. I would describe it as a bit sloppy and not according to conventional wisdom.

This process of Fijian juice vending is a good way to describe how God dispenses grace through us. It is often a bit sloppy and perhaps not up to what we have been taught to expect. Conventional wisdom would often argue that we are not to give out God's kind of love in this sloppy and even risky way. However, we serve an unconventional God. His principles never change, but He has a unique way of delivering those principles so they refresh and satisfy. The challenge for us becomes, will we be the kind of grace dispensers that people can risk trusting, regardless of what they think or have experienced.

A Difference Maker

This book was never intended to be about me or you. It was always about the people God has entrusted us with to be trained and equipped for the work of the ministry. It was about how to do this task with excellence and success. It was about becoming more like Christ in every way… just a little bit more each day. Underlying all you have read, is my desire to inspire and inform you so you will be well able to share yourself and what God has put inside you, as you become a difference maker for God and His kingdom.

In Chapter 2, I wrote about my opportunity to shape my young warriors in the church in Fiji. I quoted Colossians 1:9-10.

> *(Colossians 1:9-10 NKJV) "For this reason we also, since the day we heard it, do not cease to pray for you, and to ask that you may be filled with the knowledge of His will in all wisdom and spiritual understanding; {10} that you may walk worthy of the Lord, fully pleasing Him, being fruitful in every good work and increasing in the knowledge of God;"*

As I said in Chapter 2, these Scriptures reveal four universal goals for the mentoring process. Now would be an appropriate time to remind you of them.

1. That they would walk worthy of the Lord
2. That their lives, their character and their hearts would be fully pleasing to Him
3. That their every good work would be fruitful - that their efforts would make a difference for the Kingdom of God

4. That each of them would progressively increase in the knowledge of God, causing them to be progressively more like Christ in character, word and deed

I made the point that mentoring could be defined as being the closest thing to Jesus you can possibly be so those you mentor can become the closest things to Jesus they can possibly be. As your life becomes a picture of these four mentoring goals, those around you will be the same. The amazing thing is, you truly can become the closest thing to Jesus your disciples will ever know. It simply takes God's kind of love, and a servant's kind of humility and selflessness. Wrap these in a commitment to your call and to those you are called to. You will experience the transforming power of God, as you will walk worthy of the Lord, fully pleasing Him, just as the Apostle Paul prayed.

I have been granted the blessing of walking with so many good people through seasons filled with challenges, struggles, and great triumphs. It has been my privilege to share their stories with you. Every time I re-read some portion of what I have written about them, I am encouraged to look ahead to see what is next for me, and when possible, for them. I eagerly await the next email or phone call reporting some new challenge they walked through or new victory they won.

> *(Ephesians 4:11-13 NKJV) "And He Himself gave some to be apostles, some prophets, some evangelists, and some pastors and teachers, {12} for the equipping of the saints for the work of ministry, for the edifying of the body of Christ, {13} till we all come to the unity of the faith and of the knowledge of the Son of God, to a perfect man, to the measure of the stature of the fullness of Christ;"*

There are many gifts given to us by the Holy Spirit. The Bible teaches us that everyone called to ministry and equipped with these gifts has the same ultimate purpose - to reproduce something of themselves that reflects something of Christ. As mentors, we are called to equip the saints for the work of the ministry. In your journey through the pages of this book, I trust you found deeper meaning to what mentoring requires of you and all it involves. At the end of each chapter I synthesized my thoughts into definitions of mentoring that grew out of the principles the stories of the people in the chapter revealed. Now it is time to bring together these definitions. Collectively, they boil down to a concise summary of what it really means to mentor someone before the Lord. Following is what I have come up with and will leave with you. Please note, this final definition is not the end of the matter, but only the beginning. I trust that as you follow your heart and the leading of the Holy Spirit, you will add much more to it.

A Final Concise Summary Definition of Mentoring

Mentoring is our intentional, sacrificial imitation and modeling of Christ and His love, in the company of those we are given to care for, lead and develop. We model and teach them what they need to know. We help them practice what they have learned. We inspire them to have the faith to achieve their destinies.

Mentoring, as a process, challenges them to embrace what they have been given, apply it fruitfully to their lives, and develop themselves into all God wants them to be. The goal of successful mentoring is that those it touches shall be forever changed - to the glory and honor of God.

Let's unpack this Final Concise Summary Definition of Mentoring. I have listed eight highlights. Take the time to consider each of them.

Mentoring is intentional.

Mentoring is deliberate, resolute, purposeful behavior. It has intelligent design and consideration behind it. It is always mindful of its goals and purposes. It does not leave events to chance but pursues the will, the ways and instructions of God.

Mentoring is consistently sacrificial.

Mentoring is behavior that costs a great deal. At times, it will require a painful nailing of your personal will and ambition to a cross of service for Christ's sake and the Gospel. It will often require you to forego self-gratification, comfort or even your dreams, so that others may find what God has prepared for them.

Mentoring is imitation or modeling of Christ.

Mentoring is more than behavior. It is submission to a transformation of identity. When people see you, they should be able to look past you to the Christ in you. It is an effort to let Jesus shine through you as you become just a little bit more like Him every day.

Mentoring is taught.

Mentoring is behavior that leads to learning. It requires the heart of a teacher from you, and the heart of a student from all those you will mentor. It works within the context of understanding the opportunities inherent within it. It provides opportunities to go places in Christ that only the mentoring door will open.

Mentoring is supervised practice.

Mentoring is a process of instruction embedded with supervised practical application. The application, when properly supervised, becomes equally as informative as the teaching. Mentoring is, to a great extent, trial and error. Mentor and student alike will rely on two things. First, they will rely on what has been proven by the application of God's Word. Second, they will rely on what has been proven through their own trials, errors and ultimately, their victories.

Mentoring is an inspiring impartation of faith.

One of the greatest things you can leave your charges is an inspiring, ever-increasing dose of faith. Make your life an intentional, sacrificial demonstration of trust that goes far beyond any emotions you may feel or any deficiencies you may have. Take yourself and all those with you past the natural boundaries we all live with. Climb the clouds and sit in heavenly places with God. Live as if all things are possible with Him because they are. Even when you do not feel it, just do it!

Mentoring is a demonstration of God's kind of love.

In the puzzle diagram, I placed God's kind of love at its base because it is the foundation of the heart of a mentor. It is the constant characteristic of a mentor's heart. It supports all the other pieces of the puzzle. It completes the picture. Other elements of mentoring may come and go, but God's kind of love must remain and be allowed to increase every day.

Mentoring is a challenge to those we mentor.

Mentoring invites those we mentor to embrace and become what we have challenged them with. Then, it provokes them to take what they embraced and became so they will bear lasting fruit with it.

Mentoring's ultimate purpose is that the people we mentor will touch God and then touch the world in ways that honor and give glory to Jesus. Let honor and glory to Him drive your purpose. Let people see Jesus in every moment of the mentoring process and more importantly, in every dimension of your life.

Look within yourself.

We have now arrived at a solid picture of who a mentor is. You will notice in the illustration of a heart-shaped puzzle, above, there are blank, unlabeled pieces. The picture is incomplete. I invite you to look within your heart. Personalize this puzzle and see what you might add or change. Add to or revise the list of highlights above. Then, reflect on what your heart's puzzle looks like. Let it speak to you. Listen to it. Learn from it. Draw strength and encouragement from it. Then, go forward, as your life fills in the blanks.

Perhaps it has not escaped you that this picture of a mentor's heart is really no different than God's design for every one of His children. He simply asks us to reproduce what He produced in us. He has charged every believer to go into all the world and make disciples. How much more for those of us who are called to the specific task of training, equipping and inspiring leaders in the church?

Consider the following.

- Are some of the things you previously thought now becoming less important or perhaps irrelevant. Why?
- Has your vision and understanding of your call to ministry changed progressively as you read through these ten chapters? Do you sense a bigger picture of your life and its purposes now that we have reached the end of the book? What will you do with what you have discovered? How will you do it?
- In what specific ways has your opinion of those you mentor (or will mentor) evolved?
- Have other questions arisen? It would be good to seek God and answer them as best you can. Perhaps as you begin to answer them, they will lead you to even more questions. That would be an excellent way to complete your reading of this work.

I started the book by sharing with you my experience in a grimy old theater my first Sunday in Fiji. My earnest desire is that what I have shared with you has touched you as profoundly as the words, "just a little bit more" touched me that day long ago. Consider what you are taking away from your time in this book. I pray that it will all add up to "just a little bit more" of God in you, and in each person you touch.

Thank you for investing your time in this book. Now that you have completed it, and have seen how I arrived at my final definition of mentoring, take the time to think through and write out for yourself, what your own personal definition of mentoring would be. Then, go out and make it real to those God gives you. Make a difference for Christ. He is worthy!

Scripture Index

	Reference	Chapter	Page
1.	Esther 4:14b	3	54
2.	Esther 5:1-3	3	56
3.	1 Kings 3:7-9	3	61
4.	2 Kings 2:11-15	5	114
5.	Job 13:15	6	123
6.	Psalm 34:8	Introduction	3
7.	Psalm 57:7	3	63
8.	Psalm 103:2-5	3	58
9.	Psalm 105:1, 3-5	3	58
10.	Psalm 112:7	3	63
11.	Psalm 118:24	9	192
12.	Psalm 119:66	8	170
13.	Psalm 139:17-18	9	199
14.	Proverbs 1:2-5	3	62
15.	Proverbs 3:5a	9	193
16.	Proverbs 12:24	3	64
17.	Proverbs 16:16	8	165
18.	Ecclesiastes 4:9-12	1	23
19.	Song of Songs 2:4	7	145
20.	Isaiah 40:10-11	6	119
21.	Isaiah 55:8-9	9	193
22.	Isaiah 59:1	6	119
23.	Jeremiah 1:12	5	113
24.	Matthew 5:14-16	9	208
25.	Matthew 5:16	4	93
26.	Matthew 5:16	7	149
27.	Matthew 7:16-20	8	180
28.	Matthew 14:14	3	60
29.	Matthew 25:23	Introduction	5
30.	Matthew 25:35a	7	149
31.	Matthew 25:35b-36	7	150
32.	Matthew 25:35-40	3	60
33.	Matthew 25:35-40	7	148
34.	Matthew 25:37-38	7	152
35.	Matthew 25:40	7	153
36.	Matthew 28:18-19	Introduction	1
37.	Mark 9:23	4	86
38.	Mark 9:23	5	113
39.	Mark 9:23	6	125

40.	Mark 9:23	6	134
41.	Mark 11:24	5	115
42.	Luke 4:18-19	7	159
43.	Luke 6:38	6	129
44.	Luke 6:45	7	154
45.	Luke 6:45	8	179
46.	Luke 9:3	7	152
47.	Luke 10:33-37	8	176
48.	Luke 17:5-6	6	134
49.	Luke 23:33-34	8	177
50.	John 3:16	7	149
51.	John 13:34-35	7	160
52.	John 15:8	5	96
53.	John 15:14-16	4	90
54.	John 15:15	9	206
55.	John 15:16	5	96
56.	John 20:28	5	104
57.	Acts 9:6	5	106
58.	Acts 20:22-24	9	194
59.	Romans 8:1	8	169
60.	Romans 8:28	5	9
61.	Romans 8:28	8	163
62.	Romans 8:28-29a	4	7
63.	Romans 8:28-29	5	103
64.	Romans 8:28-29	9	207
65.	Romans 12:1-2	Introduction	5
66.	Romans 15:5	1	18
67.	1 Corinthians 4:15	2	25
68.	1 Corinthians 11:1	4	83
69.	1 Corinthians 13:8	1	11
70.	1 Corinthians 13:8a	7	151
71.	1 Corinthians 13:8b	2	33
72.	1 Corinthians 15:57-58	3	63
73.	2 Corinthians 5:9	4	91
74.	2 Corinthians 5:17	5	110
75.	2 Corinthians 5:17	5	98
76.	Galatians 2:20	7	151
77.	Ephesians 1:18	2	33
78.	Ephesians 2:4-5	3	66
79.	Ephesians 2:8-9	1	21
80.	Ephesians 4:11-13	10	214
81.	Ephesians 6:13	3	44
82.	Philippians 2:3, 5-8	5	105
83.	Philippians 3:7-8	9	193

84.	Colossians 1:9-10	2	29
85.	Colossians 1:9-10	2	33
86.	Colossians 1:9-10	3	41
87.	Colossians 1:9-10	3	68
88.	Colossians 1:9-10	10	213
89.	1 Timothy 1:2a	4	71
90.	2 Timothy 1:2a	4	71
91.	2 Timothy 2:1-2	1	15
92.	2 Timothy 2:15	5	102
93.	2 Timothy 2:20-23	8	174
94.	2 Timothy 3:14	2	45
95.	Titus 1:4a	4	71
96.	Hebrews 11:6	6	124
97.	Hebrews 11:6	9	203
98.	James 1:2	9	198
99.	James 1:2-4	6	135
100.	1 John 1:9	2	37
101.	1 John 2:9-11	7	141
102.	1 John 3:18	7	154
103.	1 John 4:7-9, 11-12	3	66

About Dr. Abramson

Dr. Abramson's ministry includes consulting, mentoring, counsel and individual coaching to senior pastors. He is active in leadership training, Bible school teaching, and preaching the Word of God around the world.

Over the years, Dr. Abramson has pastored multicultural, international churches including those in New York City and the Fiji Islands in the South Pacific. He previously established or taught in Bible schools and ministry training centers in New Zealand, Fiji, Taiwan, Hong Kong, Malaysia, Europe and the United States.

Dr. Abramson serves as an adjunct professor for New Covenant International University, supervising seminary students' in their masters and doctoral studies. He conducts seminars in pastoral training, pastoral practices, church leadership, men's ministry, marriage enrichment and recovery from broken relationships and damaged emotions. He has authored extensive curriculum materials for ministry training, including this book and its accompanying workbook.

Dr. Abramson has earned three fully accredited American theological degrees: a Doctor of Ministry from Erskine Theological Seminary, with a concentration on supra-cultural marriage and family issues; a Masters in Religion from Liberty University; and a Bachelor of Arts in Bible with a minor in Systematic Theology from Southeastern University. He currently resides with his wife Nancy in Lake Worth, Florida. They have five grown children and five grandchildren.

If you wish to contact Dr. Abramson, please visit
www.mentoringministry.com

Made in the USA
Charleston, SC
09 February 2012